SPIRITUALITY OF CREATION, EVOLUTION, AND WORK

Past Light on Present Life:
Theology, Ethics, and Spirituality

Roger Haight, SJ, Alfred Pach III,
and *Amanda Avila Kaminski,* series editors

These volumes are offered to the academic community of teachers and learners in the fields of Christian history, theology, ethics, and spirituality. They introduce classic texts by authors whose contributions have markedly affected the development of Christianity, especially in the West. The texts are accompanied by an introductory essay on context and key themes and followed by an interpretation that dialogically engages the original message with the issues of ethics, theology, and spirituality in the present.

Spirituality of Creation, Evolution, and Work

CATHERINE KELLER
AND PIERRE TEILHARD DE CHARDIN

EDITED AND WITH COMMENTARY BY
Roger Haight, SJ, Alfred Pach III,
and *Amanda Avila Kaminski*

FORDHAM UNIVERSITY PRESS   NEW YORK 2023

This series has been generously supported by a
theological education grant from the E. Rhodes
and Leona B. Carpenter Foundation.

Contents

SPIRITUALITY OF CREATION, EVOLUTION, AND WORK

I

Introduction to the Authors and the Texts

This unlikely dialogue between two thinkers so far apart revolves around things that intensely concern each of them. They share basic commitments to, for example, a metaphysics of becoming, the inner bonding and inseparability of spirit and matter, a mystical sensibility, and an activist spirituality. The fact that they approach these aspects of reality so differently, from diverse cultures, times, life-stories, Christian denominations, and disciplines only makes their convergence more remarkable and credible.

The implicit conversation between Catherine Keller and Pierre Teilhard de Chardin begins with an introduction to each author, and, in the light of certain key ideas, it offers a first look in the direction that the texts point.

Catherine Keller

Catherine Keller currently teaches theology in the Graduate Division of Religion at Drew University. Her educational background communicates a sense of how she developed and helps to locate her in today's theological conversation.

Keller's theological development. Catherine Keller was born in 1953 and, after high school, completed a program with a major in theology at the University of Heidelberg in 1974. She then took up theological studies at Eden Theological Seminary, a United Church of Christ seminary outside of St. Louis. She graduated from Eden with an MDiv in 1977. Fully committed to the study of theology, she took up a program in the philosophy of religion and theology at Claremont Graduate School, where she finished her doctoral studies in 1984.

Keller wears several self-descriptions as an academic, but one would not be wrong in beginning with her identity as a process theologian. Her work has been influenced by the process thought of Alfred North Whitehead and his conception of the dynamic interrelations that account for all things and the structure of being itself. As a feminist theologian, she weaves the themes of equality and just relationships into her theological judgments. She is acutely aware that things are always changing and that context intrinsically affects understanding. She self-describes as a critical and constructive theologian who tries to make the tradition meaningful in the time and place of its proclamation.

Keller has been teaching at Drew University for over thirty years in Drew's Graduate Division of Religion. She has a broad interdisciplinary outlook and competence. Her many books deal with basic issues in theological understanding from a perspective that is simultaneously cosmological, socially ethical, and appreciative of the depth and transcendence of reality. She communicates a certain urgency about the new exigencies that ecological destabilization has imposed on us.

Reconstructing theology on the basis of relation and process. Several vital ideas help characterize Keller's thinking and connect her in a distinct way to the topic of Christian spirituality. Three stand out and connect her indirectly to the thought of Teilhard: the basic premise of process or becoming, the understanding that the idea of creation should not be understood as an act that happened in the past but as an ongoing process, and the strong bond between matter and spirit. These ideas course through much of her work. Because she works from a perspective of a metaphysics of becoming, her writing sets up an imaginative framework for situating the scientifically mediated thought of Teilhard. What follows uses these ideas as a plan for bringing out the character of process and becoming that is found in the short composite text of Keller that follows.[1] These ideas also open up the interrelated character of all reality. The aim here is to show the complementarity between process and evolutionary thinking, the dialogical character of this present-day theologian, and the congruity of her thought to the otherwise very different work of Teilhard de Chardin on the Christian life.

(1) Process theology. From the beginnings of the Christian movement, as the church spread across widely separated cities of the Mediterranean Sea, the leaders worried about the fragmentation of the Christian message by cultural diversity. In a classical world, change means loss of identity and ultimately loss of truth. But what if the very character of reality consists of temporal change? How would a community preserve past meaning and relate it to changing and thus always new situations? Keller's response to this basic problem is twofold: appropriate the present-day world into one's thinking and make sure, constructively, that the truths of tradition are always reaffirmed in relation to the context that they are presently addressing. Process theology sets a contextual ideal for truth: it must be arrived at interrelationally—that is, within the mix of myriad relationships. The correlate of this is conversation among many different points of view. As things are related to each other and interact, so too should theology as a discipline mirror reality and be conceived as involving an exchange between constituencies about the past as it relates to the present and the future.[2]

(2) Creation theology. Keller approaches creation theology through commentary on the creation story of Genesis. Although she also has a scientific and a philosophical interpretation of creation, she proposes an aesthetic symbolic account of imagining chaos, the abyss, as infinite potentiality that God works into meaningful coherence. She calls this a process of *"creatio ex profundis"* so that, while God empowers from within, divine influence also empowers "us to participate in it actively, indeed, interactively."[3] Creation is not an act of God completed in the past but the ongoing power of God that, from within, dynamically sustains reality as transcendent power within the chaos of possibility.

(3) The non-duality of spirit and matter. Keller's reflection on creation results in a cosmology called "panentheism" because the deep structure of reality entails its subsisting in the power of God. This places God within all reality as its empowering divine Spirit. "Such radical incarnationalism does not diminish the distinction between the material world and divine mystery but rather intensifies the open-ended interaction between them."[4] Panentheism in Keller's thinking proposes an inseparable unity between God as Spirit and matter so that they coexist and mutually codetermine actual existence. "Spirit matters" because it materializes itself into the physical.

In sum, with these three organizing concepts, the given of a universe in process, a theology of ongoing creation happening within the movement, and a non-dual inseparability of matter and spirit, Keller lays out the groundwork for a spirituality of everyday life that covers all human activity. It bestows ultimate value on present-day work. It reinterprets the destructive idea of human dominion over the world: "How could dominion in the con/text of Genesis 1 mean anything but to *call this gifted and aggressive earthling to responsibility?*"[5] The short text of Catherine Keller thus sets up a framework for an active spirituality that unfolds within an ongoing creative evolutionary world and attributes spiritual value to human work.

Pierre Teilhard de Chardin

Pierre Teilhard de Chardin is rarely identified as a process theologian, but his scientific outlook led him to adopt an evolutionary framework that contributed to what today is called "process thinking." This will become apparent in the account of the development of his thought, certain important conceptual touchstones for deciphering the texts, and a preliminary foreshadowing of his conception of Christian spirituality.

The life and development of Teilhard's thought.[6] Teilhard was born in central France in 1881 outside of Clermont-Ferrand, the fourth of eleven children. At ten he was sent to a Jesuit boarding school, and at eighteen, in 1899, he joined the Jesuits. He had a scientific bent, and during his study of theology in preparation for his ordination in 1911 he was inspired by Henri Bergson's *Creative Evolution*. His studies were interrupted by the war when, in early 1915, he reported for duty as a noncombatant stretcher bearer. In 1922 he received his doctorate in geology at the Institut Catholique in Paris and formally became an assistant professor there.

During these years Teilhard had published spiritual reflections that attracted the attention of church officials. The leaders of the Catholic Church were hypersensitive during the decades following the condemnation of "Modernism" in 1907. After a sojourn in China working as a paleontologist between 1923 and 1924, Teilhard returned to Paris to find that his thought was suspect. The issue was evolution. This was the beginning of official Catholic suppression of his thought, which lasted until his death.

Between 1926 and 1946 Teilhard's base was China, where he moved about and from where he traveled widely. He wrote

The Divine Milieu in 1926–27. His most celebrated work is *The Phenomenon of Man.*

After World War II, Teilhard moved back to Paris in 1946. Exhausted, he had a heart attack in 1947 but recovered and was able to do a mission to South Africa supported by the Wenner-Gren Foundation, which sponsored work in anthropology. He continued scientific work with the foundation after his move to New York in 1951. He died on April 10, 1955, Easter Sunday, and is buried in a Jesuit cemetery in Poughkeepsie, New York.

Basic ideas of Teilhard. In lieu of reading an introduction to the thought of Teilhard de Chardin, one can gain a basic feel for his distinctiveness by calling up a few ideas that contribute to the presuppositions of his writing. The choice of the distinctions that follow are determined by their relevance to the texts from *The Divine Milieu* and to his identity as a Christian author.

(1) All reality is becoming and emergent. This phrase describes a fundamental conception of Teilhard about the nature of created reality itself. It had many roots and could be called a metaphysical position from a philosophical perspective, or a scientific conviction, or an experiential view that was gradually internalized. According to Ursula King, "It was at Hastings . . . that Teilhard discovered the meaning of evolution for the Christian faith after reading Bergson's influential book *Creative Evolution.* The theory of evolution made him see the natural and human world very differently; it made him realize that all becoming is immersed in an immense stream of evolutionary creation where every reality is animated by a 'christic element.'"[7] Teilhard de Chardin stated it directly and plainly: "Everything is the sum of the past and . . . nothing is comprehensible except through its history. 'Nature' is the equivalent of 'becoming,' self-creation: this is the view to which experience irresistibly leads us."[8]

(2) The thoroughgoing immanence of God. Teilhard's conception of God was not "up there" or "out there." God was

within reality. Teilhard was not a pantheist, even when some phrases might have sounded like it; he was not an animist. He rather had a sense that God suffused all of reality. One could call him a panentheist today, but the term did not exist in his vocabulary. During his military service he wrote of God as follows:

God is vibrant in the ether; and through the ether he makes his way into the very marrow of my material substance. Through him, all bodies come together, exert influence upon one another, and sustain one another in the unity of the all-embracing sphere, the confines of whose surface outrun our imagination. God is at work within life. He helps it, raises it up, gives it the impulse that drives it along, the appetite that attracts it, the growth that transforms it. I can feel God, touch him, "live" him in the deep biological current that runs through my soul and carries it with it.[9]

He picks this up in *The Divine Milieu*: the "God whom we try to apprehend by the groping of our lives—that self-same God is as pervasive and perceptible as the atmosphere in which we are bathed. He encompasses us on all sides, like the world itself."[10]

(3) The teleological character of reality. Teilhard reflexively accepted the teleological character of the flow of reality and the direction set by a process of complexification. The source of this conviction probably lay in his Catholic Christian faith. Consider the first theme of the first Spiritual Exercise of Ignatius Loyola, to which Teilhard would have been exposed in his early schooling and on which he meditated every year of his Jesuit life: "Human beings are created to praise, reverence, and serve God our Lord, and by means of this to save their souls."[11] This framework for perceiving and interpreting reality draws from a source that is prior to and deeper than empirical evidence can yield. It is likely that Teilhard

prepossessed this faith-based metaphysical outlook, so that it disposed him to read the experience of God's presence within the formation of the universe, the planet, its strata of living things leading to human self-consciousness in a teleological way. What sometimes sounds like a scientific basis of his conception of the ascent of reality makes more sense as convergence of appearances with an energetic and vital vision of faith.[12]

(4) Anthropocentrism. Underlining this quality of Teilhard's thinking is not meant in opposition to the Christocentrism that follows or to the role of God in Teilhard's imagination. It rather serves to highlight the important focus on human agency in Teilhard spirituality. His spirituality, like his life, was activist; his mystical sensibilities and experiences of divine immanence and presence augment rather than diminish his active life. The human spirit is presently the high point of the evolutionary development on this home planet, and through human agency human existence will ascend to further plateaus. The subject matter of Teilhard's spirituality then comes to a focus on self-conscious or intentional human activity.[13]

(5) Christocentrism. Christocentrism in Teilhard's writing refers to "a deep, intimate, and extraordinarily vibrant love of Christ—the human Jesus and the Christ of the cosmos, the ever greater, ever-present Christ, the touch of whose hands we encounter deeply within all things. Teilhard's spirituality is animated by a fervent pan-Christic mysticism."[14] Teilhard awards the actions of God in the world to Christ in an overt way, relying on texts found in Colossians that describe a cosmic Christ. "He is the image of the invisible God, the first-born of all creation; for in him all things were created. . . . He is before all things, and in him all things hold together" (Col 1:15–17). Teilhard writes, "By the universal Christ, I mean Christ the organic center of the entire universe. . . . *Of the entire universe*, . . . the center not only of moral and religious effort, but also of all that that effort implies—in other words of all physical and spiritual growth."[15]

Teilhard's "mysticism" at this point refers to the intimate and personal character of experience that characterizes his totalizing language about the role of Christ in the world. The language reflects a kind of experience that transforms the objective doctrinal language into the living framework of his existential life.

These ideas, boldly stated like theses, together reflect a large spiritual and cognitive apperceptive framework for encountering the world. They describe a passionate spiritual writer who self-consciously thinks in a Christocentric way and lays out the metaphysical place of humanity in the universe. His world is flooded with God's presence, symbolized as either Spirit or Christ, fully supporting human activity from within and indirectly from without through nature and society. He perceives reality as moving, dynamically guided by God within, toward its goal of becoming all-in-all in God. Humanity has been given the role of the conscious collective agents of this movement.

Christian life in an evolutionary world. Teilhard divides his understanding of an activist spirituality in an evolutionary context into two parts, human activities and passivities. These represent what people do and what is done to them, what they control and what they "suffer." Beginning with activity, one can discern the basic structure of his argument and the kernel of how Teilhard views these two dimensions of Christian spiritual existence.

(1) Life's activity. Teilhard casts a dim view of the spirituality of a pure intention that was emphasized by Cassian in his theology of monastic life. He charges it with initiating a divide between spiritual intent and concrete work, one that minimizes worldly activity and devalues the material world. A larger evolutionary cosmology generates new insight into anthropology. Just as the emergent process of evolution has given shape to a bewildering unity of intricately complex material interrelationships, so too each person replicates this process in one's own person. "In each one of us, through matter,

the whole history of the world is in part reflected."[16] Each person constructs the self, and something greater than himself or herself, from the material world; each one is a source of an increment in being.

Teilhard merges his conception of the creativity of human activity with the kingdom of God that Jesus preached. All our actions are contributing infinitesimally to the building up of the kingdom of God, which Teilhard conceives in both spiritual and material terms. "Owing to the interrelation between matter, soul and Christ, we bring part of the being which he desires back to God *in whatever we do*."[17] Each person plays a part in the cosmic drama.

This insertion of existential human activity into the framework of a cosmic process of evolution has several consequences for routine issues that are involved in Christian spirituality. To the question of personal salvation and unity with God Teilhard says, "To begin with, in action I adhere to the creative power of God; I coincide with it; I become not only its instrument but its living extension. And as there is nothing more personal in a being than his will, I merge myself, in a sense, through my heart, with the very heart of God."[18] This responds on the most foundational level to a conception of how a person is united with God: surely by a union of wills actualized by one's behavior. But much more: he conceives something like a process of co-creation.

In the larger purview of ultimate salvation, Teilhard combines a firm teleological notion of evolution's direction with a decisive place that human existence holds as the carrier of the world into the future. Human beings are charged with the task of being the new reflectively conscious mediators of God's intentions for all reality.

This grand conception of things offers an encompassing relevance for the actions of a person of faith. Beyond "sanctification through fulfilling the duties of our station"[19] and cementing their relationship with God, human beings are contributing to the end-time. This conviction doubles back to provide a conviction that all persons can contribute their personal efforts and participate in a project of absolute importance. Teilhard's vision thus validates each person's life and can provide each one with a strong sense of his or her value.[20]

(2) Life's passivity. Teilhard defines passivities as what are undergone. They bear some resemblance to what Paul Tillich calls destiny, the given limits of being, in polar tension with freedom. Passivities refer to all that nature has provided us. They make up by far the largest dimension of human existence, the ocean out of which a person's singular freedom emerges. Together they resemble the darkness of night in which the beams of liberty and reflection shed a small radius of light. These passivities lead human beings in two different directions: some push toward development, others toward decline. Passivities thus appear to be both friendly and hostile to human existence and growth. Teilhard therefore distinguishes between the forces of growth and the forces of diminishment.[21]

Both sets of passivity, those that support growth and those that seem to attack the human person, can be classified again in the two distinct ways of those within and those working on us from outside ourselves. Teilhard calls the inside and outside dimensions of human dependence the two hands of God. God supports the being of each individual directly by creation; God also provides support for existence by creating the environment that shores up each person.

Looking inward, God supports human beings as continual creator. Human beings are absolutely dependent upon God, inside, for their very being. God is the source and sustainer of human existence, of who and what each one is; all human capabilities and individual talents share a quality of gift; as parts of us, they are given to us, and we are not responsible for them.

Then, looking outward, one finds all the historical and social forces that have shaped the person and continue to define a person's present moment and immediate future. The mind reels at the thought of the number of factors that "must coincide at every moment if the least of living things is to survive and to succeed in its enterprises."[22] Teilhard prayerfully reflects on these two vectors constituting every life as an individual. The whole of a being and its inner shape are constantly supported by the totality of external agencies of worldly existence: the "double thread of my life."[23]

God is more easily discerned in the passivities of growth than in diminishments. But all persons have to be able to deal with decline, whether it attacks from without or works inside them. The *external misfortunes* are all the events that block our way. A clear example is Job, whose possessions were stripped away. These are tragic interruptions of life that break in on everything from carefully laid plans to the basic direction of one's path. Frequently, external misfortunes can be redressed; possessions can be regained.[24] By contrast, the *internal passivities of diminishment* are more ruthless. These are the many limitations in personal being: human will, intelligence, or bodily functions. They take the form of so many possible illnesses. Time itself excels as the most corrosive agent of all, pushing relentlessly toward physical death.

How can God be found at this interior and ontological level? Teilhard distinguishes "two phases, two periods, in the process which culminates in the transfiguration of our diminishments. The first of these phases is that of our struggle against evil. The second is that of defeat and of its transfiguration."[25] They are in a way commonsensical. The first reaction to death, not only in the self but all around, is resistance. "At the first approach of the diminishments we cannot hope to find God except by loathing what is coming upon us and doing our best to avoid it. The more we repel suffering at that moment, with our whole heart and our whole strength, the more closely we cleave to the heart and action of God."[26]

The second phase comes at the end, when one must resign oneself to death, when one can no longer resist. "God must, in some way or other, make room for himself, hollowing us out and emptying us, if he is finally to penetrate into us."[27] But this resignation can only come "*when all my strength is spent, at the point where my activity, fully extended and straining towards betterment . . . finds itself continually counter-weighted by forces tending to halt me or overwhelm me.*"[28]

*   *   *   *

One can see at this point how the lineaments of spirituality from Keller's process thought and Teilhard's evolutionary perspective converge at several junctures. From different disciplinary commitments they fix on the inner structure of reality's continual incremental becoming. Their theologies of creation come to a focus on the creativity that is actually going on in the present life of each person. Reflecting on the human relationship with God, both find transcendent God within the material universe. These two elements, immersion in the process of material becoming and finding God by consciously participating in that process, result in a certain "sacralization" of matter. As Teilhard puts it, "By virtue of the Creation and, still more, of the Incarnation, *nothing* here below *is profane* for those who know how to see."[29] Both of these thinkers draw the creativity of human beings and the work that they do into the heart of spirituality.

Notes

1. The texts representing Catherine Keller's contribution to the conversation are drawn from chapters 1 and 3 of Keller, *On the Mystery: Discerning God in Process* (Minneapolis: Fortress, 2008). They discuss the nature of theology, particularly as process thought, and the mystery of God's creating.

2. Ibid., 22.

3. Ibid., 48.

4. Ibid., 53.

5. Ibid., 66.

6. A brief biography of Teilhard de Chardin, written by John Grim and Mary Evelyn Tucker, may be found at http://teilhardde chardin.org/index.php/biography. See also a detailed timeline of his life at http://teilharddechardin.org/index.php/timeline.

7. Ursula King, ed., *Pierre Teilhard de Chardin: Selected Writings* (Maryknoll, N.Y.: Orbis, 1999), 14.

8. Pierre Teilhard de Chardin, *The Future of Man* (New York: Doubleday, Image, 1964), 3. This was written in Paris on August 10, 1920.

9. Pierre Teilhard de Chardin, *Writings in Time of War* (New York: Harper & Row, 1968), 61.

10. Pierre Teilhard de Chardin, *The Divine Milieu: An Essay on the Interior Life* (New York: Harper Torchbooks, 1960), 46.

11. Ignatius Loyola, *The Spiritual Exercises of Saint Ignatius*, ed. George E. Ganss (Chicago: Loyola Press, 1992), no. 23.

12. This responds to Stephen Toulmin's criticism that Teilhard, who was neither a trained theologian nor a critical philosopher, but was a scientist trained in geology and paleontology, failed to establish his position on teleology with scientific warrant or evidence; he thus has no place in public intellectual discourse; Toulmin, "On Teilhard de Chardin," *Commentary* (March 1965), https://www.commentarymagazine.com/articles/stephen-toulmin/on-teilhard-de-chardin/. Teilhard's genre of argumentation is a complex hybrid, but he was enough of a theologian to know that the object of one's faith, be it religious or agnostic, cannot be established scientifically.

13. Teilhard wrote before the now common sensibility that nature is not a limitless domain for human exploitation. One does not perceive in his writing today's urgency for responsibility in curtailing human dominance over nature and reverential sensibility for other aspects of our physical habitat and communion with other forms of life.

14. King, *Teilhard de Chardin*, 18.

15. Pierre Teilhard de Chardin, *Science and Christ* (New York: Harper & Row, 1968), 14.

16. Teilhard de Chardin, *Divine Milieu*, 59.

17. Ibid., 62.

18. Ibid., 62–63.

19. Ibid., 65.

20. "So, gradually, the worker no longer belongs to himself. Little by little the great breath of the universe has insinuated itself into him through the fissure of his humble but faithful action, has broadened him, raised him up, borne him on"; ibid., 72.

21. Ibid., 75–76.
22. Ibid., 78.
23. Ibid., 80.
24. Ibid., 81.
25. Ibid., 83.
26. Ibid., 84.
27. Ibid., 89.
28. Ibid., 92.
29. Ibid., 66.

II
The Texts

Catherine Keller: On Process Thinking

Selections from *On the Mystery:*
Discerning Divinity in Process

From Chapter 1: Come, My Way

Theology as Process

Calling "God"

What would it mean to do theology as an *open system*? Theology as an academic and church discipline is usually referred to as "systematic," suggestive of a majestic architecture of doctrines, a medieval cathedral of the mind. Without losing the gothic brilliance of the discipline, let us recognize the dilemma. The very word *theology* seems to yank our gaze upward, away from the pain of abused persons, away from our intimate or public passions, away from the adventures and misadventures of our embodied lives, here, now.

Theology: bits of an old creed echo through our brain: I believe in God the Father Almighty, Maker of Heaven and Earth, and in Jesus Christ his only begotten son . . . born of the Virgin Mary. . . . All vivid images, snatched from the biblical story. Their familial resonances may strike us as meaningful and indispensable, as beautiful in their antiquity, as patriarchal pontifications, or as childish nostalgia, kitschy among adults. But whatever emotional coloration they may have for us, they condense wide systems of thought and lively biblical narratives into compact abstraction.

Theological language is an odd mix: of vivid story-characters extracted from scripture and the most cosmically stretched ideas from ancient Greek philosophy onward. I love this mix. But it is complex—and dangerous, when we neglect its complexity. From the rich and messy set of narratives comprising the Bible, certain metaphoric themes were lifted up, repeated, generalized—a process of abstraction beginning to happen within the Bible itself, at least in Paul's writing, touched by Greek Stoic philosophy. Abstraction is a necessary part of any reflective process. But by means of these abstractions, stories have been often dogmatically pounded into simple propositions of belief. These abstractions are convenient. But they too easily mask the complex mix of metaphor, history, and philosophy. Indeed, they may disguise the metaphors as pseudo-facts.

When we forget that these metaphors are metaphors, when we think, for instance, that the metaphor of "God the Father Almighty" refers in a direct and factual way to an entity up there, we are committing what the philosopher of process, Alfred North Whitehead, called "the fallacy of misplaced concreteness."[1] Those concrete attributes of fatherhood refer to the particular experiences of biological fathers within the context of a monotheistic patriarchy, in which an "almighty" deity could of course only be imagined as masculine. The fallacy lies in confusing the concreteness of metaphors derived from a particular, finite historical context with the infinity we may call—for want of a better word— "God." *Literalism* is the simple word for this fallacy. It freezes theology into single meanings. Instead of flowing from an inexhaustible truth-*process*, meaning gets trapped in a truth-*stasis*.

Words strain,
Crack and sometimes break, under the burden,
Under the tension, slip, slide, perish,

Decay with imprecision, will not stay in place,
Will not stay still.

—T. S. Eliot[2]

Yet mystery is itself not absolute. Otherwise, we would have nothing to say. And that is why we use metaphors of all sorts in theology: to realize our relationship to the mystery. To realize it in language: to *speak* God's *sophia* in a mystery. But in such speech, words, as Eliot says, "strain/Crack and sometimes break under the burden. . . ." Scripture is littered with broken words, words breaking open new meanings, breaking open closed systems. The Bible brims with metaphor, trope, figure of speech, parable, psalm, prayer, story. When abstract propositions of belief (like "Jesus Christ is our Lord and Savior" or "I believe in the triune God") that are rare in scripture become fixed in a closed system, the fallacious factualism kicks in. The propositions then draw our concern *away* from the concrete processes of our shared creaturely life, rather than spiritually illumining them. Metaphors (like the Christ, Lord, Savior, Trinity, and so forth) then lose their metaphoric valency, their open-ended interactivity: for metaphors are language in process, not in stasis.

The metaphors are ground down into changeless truths when the *ab*straction makes itself *ab*solute: those terms mean almost the same thing in their Latin root: both signify a "drawing away from," a separation. When that separation is absolute it becomes irreversible; the abstraction frees itself of reciprocity with the bodily world. Thus an absolute truth is deemed nonrelative to anything else, *ab*solved of all interdependence, all conditions, all vulnerability, all passion, all change. Those with some theological training will recognize the abstract (and surprisingly nonbiblical) features of the God of classical theism.

But what if that sort of changeless stasis is not even what God—let alone the creation—*means*? What if "God" did not first and need not now mean some super-entity up there in an abstract heaven, invulnerably transcendent of time and its trials? Scripture has no such notion. Its metaphors suggest a transcendence of qualitative difference but not of dispassionate immutability. But, of course, the Bible virtually never gives any abstract definition of God. One of the (two) times it seems to, it announces, "God is love" (1 John 4:16). Does this suggest some changeless and dispassionate paternal entity? Or rather a mystery of infinite relationship?

And yet the metaphors of this love, in its inexhaustible interactivity, got frozen twice over: in the abstractions of a changeless omnipotence on the one hand, and the stereotypes of a literal and literally masculine Person on the other. "He" appears (and for this book the masculine article will be used strictly in historical citation or in present irony) at once chillingly distant and intrusively present: an absolute masculine infinity can combine with the violently loving interventions. Of course, some can catch subtler meanings behind the popular clichés of a God-man who "comes down," presumably from Heaven Up There, dons a birthday suit, and after gamely sacrificing himself "for our sins" soon gets beamed up again. . . . But far too many thoughtful people, through too much early exposure to the Big Guy in the Sky, develop life-long God allergies.

Allergic reactions, I hear, can only be treated with a bit of the original allergen. In other words, the literalisms of God-talk can be cured not by atheism but by an alternative theology. What, however, would such a therapy for secularists have to do with the needs of people of faith? For communities of faith will naturally and necessarily speak in their own traditional codes; they will play what Wittgenstein called "language games," with their own peculiar grammars and rules of communication nowhere more apparent than in the liturgy. But I have come to trust that members of these communities must not be insulated from their own doubts. Their doubts will only deepen if they are protected from the solvents of secular relativism. Particularly when it comes to the leaders and the thinkers among communities of faith, they will find that they share something of the allergic reaction; they are inevitably, for good and for ill, immersed in a secular culture. Both its habitual nihilism and its healthy skepticism are part of us all. For the sake of our own honesty and therefore our own confidence, indeed the confidence of our testimony, we need the breathing room of a theology in process. We need its adventure and its guidance. This is not a way of what is Sunday-schoolishly called "learning about God." But it is a way of discerning divinity in process. In the process of our open-ended, on-the-ground interactions, a theology of process, itself open-ended and interactive, discerns a process and an interactivity that it may also call "God."

Anselm classically defined theology as *fides quaerens intellectum*—"faith seeking understanding." Not faith that already understands and so no longer needs to seek. That would by definition no longer be theology. Theology is not itself the faith but its quest. If we stop seeking, we are no longer *on the way*. Faith seeking understanding has then turned into "belief that understands." It then closes down the very root of *quaerens*, from which come both *question* and *quest*. Speaking the divine wisdom in a mystery, theology remains a work of human speech. Theology is not the same as faith or belief, but a disciplined and relational reflection upon them. God calls, but we are responsible for what we call "God." And God may be calling us to that very responsibility!

Can an open-systems theology, operating as it must in the third space beyond the absolutes of rigidified metaphors and the dissolutes of mere repudiation, set theology itself back on the mystery? Or does any *theology as such* presume too much? What does the faith that seeks already presume? As a theological process, faith is of course somehow *in* God.

"God"! As *theos-logos*, God-talk, theology cannot take its first step without a leap of faith: if not into an entire apparatus of dogmatic answers, into a discourse in which the *name* of God already shapes our questions. So after all does God-talk always solve the mystery before it even starts?

Speaking of the Mystery

> So be silent and do not chatter about God; for when
> you chatter about him, you are telling lies and
> sinning. . . .

—Meister Eckhart[34]

Is it possible that the very name *God* endangers the mystery
that it names? The practice of not pronouncing the name of
GXD, yet writing it as the tetragrammaton YHWH,[4] answered
over two millennia ago to this paradox. In more casual speech,
Jewish tradition began early to use a delightful nickname for
the mystery: the unnamable One is addressed as *Ha Shem*—
"The Name"![5] Sixteen centuries ago, Augustine put it perfectly: *Si comprehendis, non est Deus*— "If you have understood, then what you have understood is not God."[6] And eight
centuries ago, another monk, the great mystic Meister Eckhart,
tried to still the knowing "chatter" of religious folk: "And do
not try to understand God, for God is beyond all understanding."[7] He was carrying on the tradition of "negative theology":
a strategy within theology, indeed within classical theology
itself, that negates any presumption or pretense of knowledge
of God. For it reminds us that, like us, all our concepts and
names are finite, creaturely language spoken by creatures,
based strictly on creaturely experience—and so radically
different from the mystery "God" names. Indeed, sometimes
the term *absolute* is used not to amplify beliefs about God
but to protect God's radical difference from all creatures—as
absolved from all "positive attributes." And just a bit later,
Nicholas of Cusa, an early Renaissance cardinal who loved
Augustine and Eckhart, characterized this tradition in its
radicality: "Therefore the theology of negation is so necessary
to the theology of affirmation that without it God would not
be worshiped as the infinite God but as creature; and such
worship is idolatry, for it gives to an image that which belongs
only to truth itself."[8]

What we call "God" is literally—*not*. The only proper name for God, from the perspective of negative theology, is the infinite: a purely negative term. Theology, however, whether in scholastic sophistication or in popular religion, is perpetually tempted to mistake the infinite for the finite names and images in which we clothe it. And this is idolatry. Idolatry of a most deceptive kind, the truth made lie: we might call it *theolatry*.

Mysticism means, as the word itself hints, not primarily special experiences or esoteric gifts, but a persistent attunement to the mystery. Every religion has its mystical tradition, its language of mystery, where words point toward the silence. These are very verbal disciplines, by which theology itself learns to check its own theolatries—not to inhibit its metaphors, its narratives, but their reification, their absolutization. These traditions cultivate discernment of the unknowable God—or of what in other traditions does not bear the name *God*. As Lao Tzu, the great Chinese mystic of the "Dao," the name for "way," put it over 2,500 years ago, the Dao that can be spoken is not the true Dao. All language is finite and creaturely, however inspired. Mystics groove on inspiration. But they rigorously negate, or as we say now, deconstruct, the absolutism that presumes to name the infinite like some person or entity over there; that knows God with any certainty, abstract or literal. They keep theology on its way. In her richly traditional theology of the divine Wisdom/Sophia, Elizabeth Johnson, for instance, shows how the classical way of negation is now crucial for challenges to exclusively masculine God-images: "No name or image or concept that human beings use to speak of the divine mystery ever arrives at its goal: God is essentially incomprehensible."[9]

Nonetheless the negative theologians of Judaism, Christianity, and Islam did not stop naming God. As Franz Rosenzweig put it, "Of God we know nothing. But this ignorance is ignorance of God."[10] To the contrary, the challenge of naming the unnamable seems to clear the space for fresh metaphors of the mystery. Cusa called this ignorance an ignorance not innocent of its own ignorance, the knowing ignorance: *docta ignorantia*. The mystics never tire of speaking of the unspeakable. The infinity of the divine generates an endless multiplicity of possible names. So the mystical traditions, with their iconoclastic edge, may help us all to discern the mystery of the infinite within the finite. It is like a depth, bottomless and eerie, that now and then boils up at the shadowy edges of our experience. *Bullitio*, "bubbling over," was Eckhart's word for the overflow of the divine into the world. At this effervescent edge theology itself is bubbling over, speaking—in burning tongues and modest metaphors—"God's *sophia* in a mystery." Or we really should just shut up.

Yet in the mystical traditions, orthodox or countercultural, God-talk is not forbidden or forbidding. Its mystery attracts. The caress of that mystery is like the touch of truth—delicate rather than abusive. But mystery becomes mystification if it inhibits the struggle to understand, if it blocks the quest. Mysticism becomes repressive if it restricts truth to the exotic experiences of an elite. Eckhart, when he tells us to stop chattering, is not telling anyone to remain silent. Nor is Karl Barth, not at all a mystic but a booming proclaimer of the Word of God, when he whimsically likens theology—properly broken speech—to "the 'old wife's' stammering." [11]

The calls to be quiet, to listen, to meditate, or to pay attention are not orders of silence or censorship. Theology needs breathing room between its words—the better to speak them! "Silence," writes Elliot Wolfson on Jewish mysticism, "is not to be set in binary opposition to language, but is rather the margin that demarcates its center." [12] Silence folds in and out of speech as breath folds in and out, inspiration and expiration, of the body. *Spirit* in Hebrew, Greek, and Latin literally means "breath."

Yet Protestantism especially has been afraid of silence, even in a worship service—as though it would swallow the Word. Odd that we in the West must turn to yoga or Zen to recover the incarnate moment-to-moment attention to our breathing. This attention was implicit in the occidental contemplative pathways. Contemplative prayer breathes beneath and beyond our theologies of misplaced concreteness.

"Such a way as gives us breath."

Attractive Propositions

Nonetheless theology routinely gets called "knowledge of God." I am suggesting that this definition smacks of the dreary theolatry. But all the -*ologies* are disciplines of knowledge, with their scholarly traditions and historical texts. Am I making theology an exception?

On the contrary, it is an arrogant exceptionalism that I am questioning. Theology as an academic discipline comprises a vast compendium of knowledge—none vaster. But this is *knowledge of its myriad texts and contexts, not of God*, their supreme symbol. This history will be important to any student of theology, especially if he or she is studying for the ministry in a historic Christian tradition. The historically anti-intellectualist, fundamentalist, or "Bible-believing" ministries have no patience with theology, and often consider it all more or less heretical. But their identification of faith with propositional beliefs—"fundamentals"—then becomes all the more absolute.

All that has been revealed, thought, understood, and re-thought is the basis and background for a faith that is still, always, seeking; but none of it adds up to the truth. Truth, like the manna, cannot be hoarded, refrigerated, or dried. It is a gift of the present and a grace of relation.

Theological truth, in other words, cannot be captured in propositions, no matter how correct. But neither does it happen *without* propositions. Theology is one hulking body of truth-*claims*, including that made by the present sentence. Theology—not the truth it seeks—comprises a shifting set of propositions, frayed and porous at the edges. Some of its propositions will *propose* more attractive, more healing and redeeming possibilities than others. To propose is not to impose—but to invite. A proposition may be more like an erotic appeal than a *compelling* argument: we get propositioned! In chapter 5 we will consider the process theological idea of the divine lure as God's invitation to each of us, at every moment, to become. Indeed, we are putting some key propositions to the test in this volume—propositions encoded in such ancient doctrinal loci of the tradition as the creation, the power, and the love of God. These will be *doctrines in process*: on trial and in movement. If these symbols do not help you think differently about what most *matters* in your life *now*—not looking back in a haze of nostalgia for the lost Plan A, nor forward to some Plan B afterlife, but *now*—they fail the test.

Theology then is a truth-process, not a set of truths. It speaks "God's *sophia* in a mystery" but *is* not that wisdom. If theology is not for you a bubbling process that helps your life *materialize* differently and gladly, its propositions have lost their life. Its metaphors have become frozen and brittle. Toss your theology on the waters.

It may come back—manifold.

Process Theology

Nothing more surely characterizes our era, which we might as well call postmodern, than awareness of multiplicity. High-speed global travel and communication confront us with an endless array of cultural and religious differences. This plurality sends some running back to the security of some absolute: *nulla salvus extra ecclesiam*—"No salvation outside of the church." And it dissipates others in a global marketplace of options: in my city you can buy dreamcatchers, hand-painted Guadalupes, plump plastic Buddhas, and a neon flashing Jesus all in one shop, on your way to do yoga after work on Wall Street. But when the many become the manifold, folded together, held in relationship, the third way is unfolding. To put this propositionally: relationality saves pluralism from relativism. Indeed, that proposition proposes something about how all propositions propose to us: they make new relationships possible, amidst the clutter of options.

> God-relatedness is constitutive of every occasion of experience. This does not restrict the freedom of the occasion. . . . It is God who, by confronting the world with unrealized opportunities, opens up a space for freedom and self-creativity.
> —John B. Cobb Jr. and David Ray Griffin[13]

For a relational theology, the multiplicity of the universe and of our own lives within it exercises profound spiritual attraction. Getting to know other religions, participating in secular movements for social justice—these count as positive theological activities, not threatening to one's own faith but clarifying and enriching. Again, only an absolutist Christianity views other inviting ways as competitors rather than conversation partners. A robust and living faith does not feel threatened by dissolution in the face of multiple possibilities. But pluralism represents a steep learning curve for the monotheistic traditions. What theologian Laurel Schneider calls "the logic of the One" has operated to abstract the divine from the manifold of metaphors and manifestations evident in each of the scriptural traditions.[14] In this book we cannot explore the intersections and differences of various religions. But we distinguish carefully between the relativism that slides toward the dissolute, offering a smorgasbord of ideas for sale—and a *discerning pluralism*.

Pluralism, if bound together with a robust relationalism, lets us build on and beyond Jeffersonian tolerance. It lets us *engage*, recognizing that we influence one another already anyway. We are willy-nilly interconnected. This has always been true, but in this century it has become obvious. For good and for ill, no creature, not even a hermit in the Himalayas or a molecule of oxygen a mile over her head, is untouched by the whole life-process of the planet.

No theology has earlier or better embraced the truth of our radically relational interdependence than has the movement called process theology. Rather than sensing in the impinging multiplicities of the world a growing threat for the Christian faith, it has recognized a bottomless gift. As Cobb and Griffin write, process thought "gives primacy to interdependence over independence as an ideal. Of course it portrays interdependence not simply as an ideal but as an ontologically given characteristic." It is the source of our mutual vulnerability as well as our fondest community. "We cannot escape it. However, we can either exult in this fact or bemoan it."[15] And it is precisely the dynamism of our interdependence, by which we constantly influence each other—flow into each other—that keeps us in process. "We influence each other by entering into each other."[16] If the world is an open-ended process of interactions, it is because we may exercise choice in the way we influence each other's becomings and the way we shape our own becoming out of the manifold of influences. We are indelibly marked by our past. We cannot escape the process of being influenced and of influencing. But we may exercise creative freedom within it.

For a growing number in this millennium, theology is of renewed interest, but only as a living and relational process, sensitive to difference. To say that theology is a process is to say that theology itself unfolds in relationship and in touch. It has always been multiple. It is unfinished, always, and on the way. But the metaphor of process only takes on this intensity because of the many decades of the tradition called "process theology."

Process theology is grounded in the cosmology of Whitehead, the early-twentieth-century mathematician who became a philosopher in order to connect the radical new insights of Einstein's relativity theory and quantum indeterminacy to our living sense of value. He announced that the primary task of philosophy must be the reconciliation of religion and science. His elaborate rethinking of the universe as one immense, living, and open-ended network of spontaneous interactions inspired the movement called process theology. It was developed early by Henry Nelson Wieman and Charles Hartshorne; John Cobb made it a systematic theology and a practical movement, with the collaboration of David Ray Griffin, Marjorie Suchocki, and the Claremont Center for Process Studies. This ecological and pluralist vision comprises a vast community of authors, teachers, clergy, and activists collectively rethinking the core values and symbols of the West. It is finding ever more spokespeople throughout Asia as well. The present book does not seek converts to process theology. But it takes part in the richly theological, political, and ecological vision of a process-relational universe.

It is perhaps becoming apparent that *theology as process* proposes something not just about the process of God-talk, but about what we mean by the name *God*. It does not negate theological absolutes *absolutely*; indeed, it is not often developed in relation to negative theology at all.[17] For it affirms an open system of theological metaphors. For process theologians, *God*, at once eternal and becoming, is a living process of interaction. In other words, the mystery may be addressed with metaphors of eros, of flow, of illimitable interactivity, of open ends and unknowable origins, of immeasurable materialization. But for process theology God does not lose the personal aspect. The infinite creativity of the universe is limited, contoured, drawn into relationship by what Whitehead called "the divine element in the universe." The impersonal infinity can be appropriately addressed with the interpersonal metaphors of the biblical God.

The language of prayer, the metaphors of mysticism, the scriptures of the world, provide various strategies for intimacy with the infinite. Theology is another such strategy of relationship, which process theologians have sought to revive within and beyond the churches. Such theology seeks to understand without abstracting ourselves from the process we seek to understand. Like quantum theory, it recognizes that the observer participates in that which s/he observes. Any theological standpoint outside of the process of the universe would be a fallacy of misplaced concreteness. To discern God in process means to discern at the same time our own participation in that process: our participation as social individuals, that is, as individuals who participate in one another and in God.

Amidst the uncertainties of our own history, we matter to this divinity whose *sophia* we utter. The interrelationships that bind all creatures together produce both risk and stability, change and conservation. The God of process theology resists stasis but also fragmentation. For the open, self-organizing complexity of the world can only develop through bonds that hold firm, that channel life and support meaning. Those who wish to protect elements of religious orthodoxy without rigidification, for example, or those who wish to protect the global environment without denying human need and natural shifts, will appreciate the refusal of predictable polarizations. A third way proposes both theory and practice for theology. Its discerning pluralism thrives in the conjunctions of spirited change with living traditions. The God of process theology, whose incarnate context is what William James called "the pluralistic universe," is the discerning pluralist *par excellence*.

> There are two principles inherent in the nature of things . . . the spirit of change and the spirit of conservation. There can be nothing real without them.
> —Alfred North Whitehead[18]

Such a Way

"We are not alone," in the words of a great twentieth-century hymn: "therefore let us make thanksgiving, and with justice, willing and aware, Give to earth and all things living, 'liturgies of care.'"[19] Theology, if it lives, expresses a liturgical cadence and care. We who are finite moments participating in an infinite process need more than our own individual inventions of meaning—even if we cannot escape the constructive process. Theology, as in Augustine's *Confessions*, is itself a kind of prayer. It breathes a prayer, like his, full of poetry, arguments, quotes, doubts, and discoveries. A text that breathes, that leaves its readers breathing room. A prayer evidently intended for a much wider readership than just God!

Once I was lost, but now I'm found: and still finding my way. "Such a Way as gives us breath"—will also keep us on the mystery. To do theology with honesty and without mystification, to "speak God's *sophia* in a mystery," is a process we will have to undertake together. Theology—if it means God-talk—is not God talking to us or through us. It is not our talk about God, like an object we could know. We talk critically and creatively about the God-talk of scripture and tradition. But theology signifies something more: theology is a way of discerning divinity in process. The process is both that of our faith seeking understanding—and of that which we seek to understand.

Theology is not a truth I already possess and can write out and deliver to you. The argument of this writing is that truth—and above all theological truth—cannot be *had*. But as the next chapter demonstrates, under the sign of truth and in a familiar scene of trial, we can take part in its process. "Willing and aware."

Between the absolute and the dissolute, arises the *resolute*. Like a gift, our confidence flows. And we take that next step. We might even board together.

We have only begun to make our connections.

Notes

1. Alfred North Whitehead, *Science and the Modern World* (New York: Macmillan/Free, 1967), 51f.

2. T. S. Eliot, "Burnt Norton," from "Four Quartets," in *Collected Poems 1909–1962* (New York: Harcourt, Brace & World, 1970), 180.

3. Meister Eckhart, "Sermon 83: Renovamini spiritu (ep. 4.23)," in *Meister Eckhart: The Essential Sermons, Commentaries, Treatises and Defense*, trans. and with introduction by Edmund Colledge and Bernard McGinn (Mahwah, N.J.: Paulist, 1981), 207.

4. Subsequent First/Old Testament biblical references in this text tend to maintain use of original Hebrew to name the character of God: YHWH and/or *Elohim*. See *The Five Books of Moses: The Schocken Bible*, vol. 1, trans. Everett Fox (New York: Schocken, 1995).

5. Based on Lev. 24:1. An Orthodox Jewish text explains *Ha Shem* thus: "So that God's name is not used in vain, it is customary to refrain from saying Adonai (the Lord) except in prayer and during the actual recitation of blessings. When reference is made to God in the course of conversation, even when quoting passages, the term HaShem (The Name) is used instead. . . . Other commonly used terms that refer to God are: HaKadosh Baruch Hu (The Holy One, Blessed Be He); Ribbono Shel Olam (Master of the Universe); Avinu She'ba Shamayim (Our Father in Heaven)"; Hayim Halevy Donin, *To Be a Jew: A Guide to Jewish Observance in Contemporary Life* (New York: Basic, 1972), 174.

6. Augustine, *Sermon 52*, c. 6, n. 16, quoted in Elizabeth Johnson, *She Who Is: The Mystery of God in Feminist Theological Discourse* (New York: Crossroad, 1992), 105.

7. Eckhart, "Sermon 83," 207.

8. Nicholas of Cusa, "On Learned Ignorance," in *Nicholas of Cusa: Selected Spiritual Writings*, trans. and intro by H. Lawrence Bond (New York: Paulist, 1997), I:86, 126.

9. Johnson, *She Who Is*, 117.

10. Franz Rosenzweig, *The Star of Redemption*, trans. William W. Hallo (New York: Holt, Rinehart and Winston, 1971), 23.

11. Karl Barth, *Church Dogmatics* II, 1, [38] in *Church Dogmatics: A Selection*, ed. G. W. Bromiley (New York: Harper Torchbooks, 1962), 84.

12. Elliot R. Wolfson, *Language, Eros, Being* (New York: Fordham University Press, 2005), 289. Regarding extralinguistic expressions, please note that this same Wolfson has kindly

permitted his painting "Cruciform" to grace the cover of *On the Mystery*.

13. John B. Cobb Jr. and David Ray Griffin, *Process Theology: An Introductory Exposition* (Philadelphia: Westminster, 1976), 29.

14. Laurel Schneider, *Beyond Monotheism: The Multiplicity of God* (London: Routledge, 2007).

15. Cobb and Griffin, *Process Theology*, 21.

16. Ibid., 23.

17. Joseph Bracken, Roland Faber, and I have drawn process theology into the proximity of negative theology.

18. Whitehead, *Science and the Modern World*, 201.

19. Brian Wren, "We Are Not Our Own," in the *New Century Hymnal* (Cleveland: Pilgrim, 1995), no. 564, written in 1987 for the tenth anniversary of the Liturgical Studies Program at Drew. Lyrics and melody by Wren, arranged by Fred Graham (Drew Theological School alumnus) for the hymnal version, copyright © 1989 Hope Publishing Company.

From Chapter 3: Be This Fish

Creation in Process

Ex Nihilo or Nihilism?

The grace of the fish lies not in escaping the watery chaos but in moving with its currents. Such grace does not transcend the water (like the absolute), nor does it drown (like the dissolute): our little fish, swimming bravely on, is an icon of the resolute! If we want to practice this oceanic grace, we need here to open the way and the channel theologically. So as Ambrose was preaching from the already ancient symbols of Genesis to his living context, we also read the currents of the beginning chaos as our *current* element.

In other words, the chaos—the turbulence, the uncertainty, the storms, and the depths of our actual life-process—is all signified by the watery deep, the *tehom*, of Genesis. And from that womby chaos, in the symbolic codes of many ancient peoples, including the Hebrews, the universe itself is born. The first creation narrative of Genesis is of course also giving perpetual birth to the biblical canon itself.

The narrative itself has long suffered from two kinds of interpretive absolutism. The literalist interpretations, unlike the Ambrosian allegory, reduce it to a bit of primitive pseudo-science. Then it lends itself to every form of religious war against secular science, whether the six-day creationism that simply junks the spacetime of astrophysics or the more so-phisticated "intelligent design" campaign that tries under-standably to resist neo-Darwinian reductionism but in doing so allies itself with the U.S. politics of fundamentalism.

Beyond the problems of biblical literalism, theology in general interprets the text as proof of God's creation of the world from absolutely nothing. Certainly, the *creatio ex nihilo* is one possible interpretation of the text and of the universe. Both testaments picture a creation through divine speech, a dramatic beginning of this universe rather than a static or cyclical creation. Theologians rightly argue that the radical novelty and contingency of the creation—as creation, and not just inert eternal stuff—sets it off from a purposeless universe. Yet theology usually then presumes that the *ex nihilo* version of the creation is the only alternative to nihilism.

But something is fishy in the history of interpretation! For we learn from biblical scholars that the *ex nihilo* doctrine has no basis in the letter of the text itself. The Bible narrates instead various versions of a more mysterious process: that of creation from the deep, known as the watery chaos. It inspires an alternative both to the absolutes of a top-down, once-for-all act of creation and to the dissolutes of a mech-anistic reductionism. The third way of an open-ended process of creation emerges in resistance to the presumption of a preprocessed creation. We may call this doctrinal alternative the *creatio ex profundis*.[1]

If in this chapter we reflect on the creation from the watery deep as a drama, big bang and all, that never stops, the im-mensity of the universe drip-drops into our every moment. As the theological tradition recognizes, the primal creativity persists: *creatio continua*. But our particular theology may either alienate us from this continuing creativity or empower us to participate in it actively, indeed interactively. The first chapter of Genesis can be locked down as a report on the absolute origin from nothing. It can be locked out as mere prescientific ignorance. But what if instead we open it up, almost like a parable, to suggest unexpected meanings for our lives in process now? As Ambrose suggests, the waters of genesis and regeneration, of creation and of new creation, are inseparable. Every beginning is a beginning-again. We begin again with the poor harassed text—over-used and under-understood, constantly being literalized and being debunked—of all beginning.

A Magnificent Mess

Try to bracket everything you've been taught about God and creation as you reread the opening verses of the Bible. Notice that there is no nothingness, but a whole lot of not-quite-somethingness.

> (1) *When* Elohim *began to create the heaven and the earth—*(2) *the earth was* tohu va bohu *and darkness was upon the face of* tehom *and* ruach *was pulsing over the face of the waters—*(3) *then* Elohim *said let there be light. . . .*

The second verse is the one of which the French Jewish translator and commentator Rashi wrote a thousand years ago, "This verse cries out, 'interpret me!'"[2] Poignant—the text itself is crying out to be interpreted, begging for what would later be called "hermeneutics." Genesis 1:2 opens close to home, but unrecognizably so.

If "earth" exists it can only be as the energy of a potential planet, its condition uninhabitable: *tohuvabohu*. That phrase, sometimes translated "waste and void" but better translated "waste and wild," was devised for its onomatopoetic rhythm and rhyme. "It is easy to specify the minimal redundancy, the initial repetition, incipient dawn above the waters of chaos;

it is the echo," writes a French philosopher of science, thinking of chaos theory. "Languages like to articulate it in various ways; tohu-bohu or brouhaha."[3] French dictionaries contain the word *tohubohu*, and French moms scold kids for making one. The playful poetic repetition of the Hebrew may be of the essence of its meaning: for matter, as we are learning from a new physics, *is* at base rhythm. Indeed, superstring theory "suggests that the microscopic landscape is suffused with tiny strings whose vibrational patterns orchestrate the evolution of the cosmos."[4] The earth *tohuvabohu* suggests a rhyme that has not yet found its reason. And that is just—the beginning.

In the third metaphoric pair of the second verse, the *ruach Elohim*, the spirit/breath/wind of God, also pulses. Remember the whirlwind of Job, and John's uncontainable spirit blowing in truth, flowing as living water. The Hebrew *mrhpht* (often translated as just "moved" or "hovered") connotes rather a spirit-rhythm as in the beating wings of a seabird, the oscillation of breath, or the ebb and flow of ocean. (Some scholars suggest that the verb *vibrate* best captures the range of its motile meanings.)[5] Flow in nature is a function not of a smooth continuous motion but of pulsation, as in the in- and out-take of breath keeping your supply of oxygen steady, as in the pump and pulse of your heart keeping your blood streaming, as in the ebb and flow of waves keeping the ocean moving.

It is the ocean that provides the primal metaphor of Genesis 1, as the *tehom*—the oceanic deep, later translated into Greek as *abyssos*, chaos. But the waters are also the more actualized sea, the *mayim*, over which the spirit vibrates, in exquisite attunement. Poetry synchs with the primal rhythm so much more effectively than our stilted propositions and theological abstractions. Or music: in the opening of Mahler's Third Symphony, a grand creation narrative in music, it is an eerie oscillation in the bass register that signifies the minimal gesture of genesis.[6]

> A careful reading of Genesis does not associate the
> formlessness, emptiness, darkness, the deep, or the
> waters with evil. . . . The creation story is a birth
> story, a story about the nativity of the earth and its
> creatures, including women and men. . . . A wildness,
> a free natural growth, is therefore part of all that
> lives.
>
> —Karen Baker-Fletcher[7]

There is surprising aquatic complexity in this brief text.
Those spirit-waters (*mayim*) seem to flow from the darker
waters of the deep, the *tehom*. Neither of these waters are
identical with the terrestrial ocean that is produced by being
divided from the deep above (an ancient cosmological picture,
somewhat egg- or womb-like, of the darkness of the night
sky and of the oceans as the two differentiated halves of the
deep). These waters express the widespread myth of a primal
chaos, an infinity of unformed and unfathomable potentiality.
However we interpret them, the *tohuvabohu* of matter and
the waters of the deep do not suggest some empty *nihil*.

If the cosmological intuition of the priestly writer of Genesis
is not primitive ignorance, just waiting to be debunked by
modern science and defended by modern fundamentalism, it
is theopoetics more than theoscience. But does it therefore
say nothing about the actual universe? Should we separate
the stuff of science from the stories of religion, like the two
halves of the deep?

What a wasted opportunity, just as science itself begins to
outgrow its modern reductionism. "Story?" asks the biologist
Stuart Kauffman. "Surely story is not the stuff of science. I'm
not so sure. . . . If story is not the stuff of science yet is about
how we get on with making our ever-changing livings, then
science, not story, must change."[8] For not everything in science can be deduced. In its postmodern mode it recognizes
itself as a model wrought of metaphors, relatively stabilized,
on whose vibrant basis rigorous hypotheses and testable

deductions can be made. Science is also on the mystery. Scientific reductionists have as difficult a time, of course, with such a paradigmatic shift as do religious absolutists. If we do not mistake the ancient biblical stories as pseudo-factual primitive science, if we do not abstract them into mere dogmas, we let the interpretive and inspiring power of the ancient stories come back into play, in our struggle to find our difficult way.

Panentheism

Yet for the peoples of the book, the goodness of creation, human and nonhuman natures together, is a nonnegotiable value. It cannot be traded against any supernatural hope. The core doctrine of Christianity, the incarnation, celebrates the embodiment of God in the world. And the Hebrew story of creation illustrates God the Spirit pulsing intimately, touchingly, upon the face of the uncreated waters. The fluidity of an emergent universe is the process of a becoming world. For a theology of becoming/*genesis* matter matters to the spirit. Spirit *matters*: it takes on flesh. It is not just a matter of the single incarnation, but of an enfleshment always and everywhere taking place, and always differently.

> [God's] goodness fills all his creatures and all his
> blessed works full, and endlessly overflows in them.
> . . . God is everything which is good, as I see, and the
> goodness which everything has is God.
> —Julian of Norwich[9]

This is the implication of Wesley's return to the mystical Christian sense that God is the spirit of the world, the *anima mundi*. "God is in all things, and . . . we are to see the Creator in the glass of every creature." From this all-presence he draws ecological as well as theological inferences: "We should use and look upon nothing as separate from God, which indeed is a kind of practical Atheism."[10] Similarly, in traditions close to process theology, the universe may be named "the body of God."[11] This is not to *identify* God as spirit with the body of the world, as in pantheism ("all is divine"). Instead, process theology speaks of "panentheism," to retrieve the classical vision that "all is *in* God." Such radical incarnationalism does not diminish the distinction between the material world and divine mystery but rather intensifies the open-ended interaction between them.

In a documentary by Bill Moyers about the greening of evangelical Christianity,[12] an Appalachian churchwoman is seen speaking at a demonstration against the coal-extraction process called "mountain top removal." This voracious destruction of an entire landscape is decried—not so surprisingly—as a desecration of God's creation. But one is startled to hear her announce, "The earth is God's body."[13]

Environmental spirituality, or ecotheology, as well as conversations with natural science, are examples of emerging ways to *re*associate theology with what matters. Might we awaken our culture from the sense that the matter at hand is some dull, opaque stuff, some lifeless and unfeeling substratum that we with our computer-like brains can manipulate however we please? The materialities of our lives—in the mysteries of the subatomic and the astrophysical energies, in the urgencies of the flesh, the subtleties of moods, the formation of social roles, the distribution of resources, the endangerment of the carrying capacity of the earth, the sacraments of the church—bespeak our most *spirited* interactions.

Genesis and Genetics

Already in the beginning, we are called to take responsibility for our worlds. In the story, we are created as collaborators in the creativity, in the image of the creator. Yet this cooperation in creation is not solely human. On the contrary, it is first of all the earth and the sea that are called to *put forth* or

bring forth the species that will inhabit them. Both earth and
sea are depicted as entities response-able to the divine invitation to generate life. "Let the earth put forth vegetation: plants
yielding seed, and fruit trees of every kind on earth that bear
fruit with the seed in it" (Gen. 1:11). And it does, with all that
botanical specificity repeated, beginning to overwhelm this
short, liturgical chapter, and insistently so. It is surely no
coincidence that the much longer *Enuma Elish* lacks any
reference to the flora and fauna of creation but leaps right
from the stars and planets to the humans, who appear alone,
created to be slaves of the gods.

> The extravagant gesture is the very stuff of creation.
> After the one extravagant gesture of creation in the
> first place, the universe has continued to deal exclu-
> sively in extravagances, flinging intricacies and colossi
> down aeons of emptiness, heaping profusions on
> profligacies with ever fresh vigor. The whole show has
> been on fire from the word go!
>
> —Annie Dillard[14]

"And God saw that it was good" (Gen. 1:13). An intuition
comes through here of divine pleasure in the results: As though
God's suggestions, the content later to be called "the word,"
and even later "the lure," have yielded not altogether predictable fruit. God *sees*, not *says*, that it is good. The element of
surprise, of real perception of something new, has been theologically too little perceived. Then "Let the waters bring forth
swarms of living creatures . . ." (1:20). So they do, those
mysterious waters, responding to zoological cues. And oh, it
is good. Once again, the earth brings forth—narrated with
more of the loving, repetitive lists of biodiversity. And that is
how the creation takes place, through the co-creative action
of the creatures: ". . . the waters dance in cocreative activity
with God."[15]

If we quit looking for an omniscient report, we may discern
in the text a quasi-evolutionary intuition into what biologists

call "emergence." The various populations thrive within the earth and the sea from which they emerge. The earth and the sea appear as super-organisms, anticipating the twentieth-century Gaia Hypothesis of the earth as a single complex ecosystem rather than just the sum of mechanisms more characteristic of modern taxonomies. They are creative creatures of integrity and responsiveness.

Is God the composer calling forth an ensemble to play with? An ensemble of ensembles? *Elohim* calls forth art, like the music of a jazz ensemble, with multiple solos and constant reintegration, with ever more complex riffs on the elemental themes, sounded in the depths. Primal themes, like $E = mc^2$ and the law of gravity, seem to express the law or *logos* of this universe. Then when biology happens, ACGT—the letters representing the four nucleic acids comprising the gene—sound the primal theme. The variations on those four will branch out into the thirty thousand genes making up the human genome (close in number and constitution to a chimp) and account for the unfathomable diversity of life. No wonder the science writer Matt Ridley cannot help exclaiming, "In the beginning was the word!"[16]

The *logos* of John 1:1, echoing the Elohimic utterance of Genesis, here becomes a metaphor for genes. If ACGT is itself a primal theme upon which we creatures riff at a collective level way beneath consciousness, is it not also a possible metaphor of the divine word? Here genesis and genetics are one. Yet only a reductionist science, imagining a deterministically programmed genome, will shut down the open-ended interactivity. As Ridley demonstrates in his aptly titled *Nature Via Nurture*, "Genes are not puppet masters or blueprints. Nor are they just carriers of heredity. They are active during life; they switch each other on and off; they *respond to the environment*."[17] Our genes not only order our potentiality but absorb the influence of formative experiences. Contrary to the nothing-buts of either genetic biology or social environment, our embodied life is an intensely relational process.

For as John 1 riffs on Genesis 1: without the word "not one thing came into being." Neither text suggests that the word is *all* that it takes! For without the co-creativity of the earth and sea and all the other creatures in the evolutionary process, this particular world would also not be made. But then we are speaking theologically, not scientifically, imagining our relationship as creatures to the creator.

Self-Organizing Creation

The creative Wisdom of all things has established marvelous and ineffable harmonies by which all things come together in a concord or friendship or peace or love or however else the union of all things can be designated.

—John the Scot[18]

The metaphor of a God who speaks, who calls, who creates intentionally, surely implies some notion of a designing intelligence. But are we then ipso facto implicated in a theology of "intelligent design" (ID)? Advocates of ID claim that complexity of the universe and of living things can only be explained by an intelligent cause, not a random process such as natural selection. While in attempting to make scientific arguments, they avoid explicit theology, "God" in the classical sense of the first cause is of course the designer. I actually agree with the ID advocates when they announce, "We are skeptical of claims for the ability of random mutation and natural selection to account for the complexity of life. Careful examination of the evidence for Darwinian theory should be encouraged."[19] A 1950s-style neo-Darwinian reduction of life to the interplay of chance and natural law is a theological conversation-stopper. Yet as Ridley suggests, such reductionism is also an increasingly marginal kind of biology. Besides, as the first chapter was at pains to communicate, the reassertion of a theological absolute is not the best response to a reductionist dissolute.

The ID proponents project the old picture of a Creator-God, sitting in heaven planning and directing the structure and course of the universe. Not only is such creationism too anthropomorphic, but it does not account for the spontaneous interactivity of the creatures with each other and with the creator. It reinscribes the notion of a supernatural master plan delivered by an omnipotent and unilateral providence. The problematic moral presuppositions of such a view of divine power, beyond its sheer noncredibility to so many thoughtful people of faith, will be the subject of the next chapter. For now suffice it to say that with its monarchical view of God, it cannot take into account the self-organizing complexity by which life in fact emerges. Such theology offers a preplanned, preprocessed creation, rather than a creation in process.

One scholar of science and religion, reflecting on the above divine commands to bring forth, suggests that God *continually creates* through self-organizing systems. Drawing on Ilya Prigogine and Stuart Kauffman in their work on the emergence of complexity and order in nonlinear systems, Ian Barbour proposes that God acts as a "structuring cause," influencing the range of possibilities within which creatures act. Many share his understanding of God as "designer of a self-organizing process."[20] Or one might privilege the biblical metaphors of divine *logos* or *sophia*, word or wisdom, to express the ancient intuition into what Whitehead, in his philosophical reconciliation of science and religion, considers God: the ground of order and novelty, offering an "initial aim" or "lure" to each emerging occasion. Rather than Intelligent Design we might speak of Creative Wisdom. The wisdom does not impose order but calls forth self-organizing complexity.

Contrary then to any vision of a linear designer-universe, the creation is not portrayed in Genesis as God's solo performance. One can only read there a process of cosmic collaboration. Not a thing-like creation but a complex interactive process is called forth: we may call it the *genesis collective*. Emerging from the mysterious *tehom*, the very matrix of differentiation, creatures become, like infants, increasingly other from the mother, capable of relationship—but never altogether separate. Genesis involves generations of forthcoming, multiplying creatures. The gathering cooperation unfolds as a rhythm, a cosmic liturgy: divine lure, creaturely improvisation, and divine reception—ooh, good!

When the level of order, of what biologists call "self-organizing complexity," reaches a new level, so does the risk of chaos! But since complexity theory teaches that creativity in the universe—the evolutionary leaps in organic versatility—emerges "at the edge of chaos," this risk also expresses the creative wisdom. The creation called forth in genesis is a *kosmos*, in the Greek sense of a decorative order. But unlike classical, symmetrical aesthetic, this cosmos unfolds an art of flows, waves, disruptions, and surprises. A disciplined improvisation is called forth in creatures—at great risk. Genesis names not a static and settled cosmos, but something more like what James Joyce playfully dubbed "chaosmos." In the interplay of formlessness and form, chaos and order, emergence and collapse, the possibilities in what process theology calls the "divine lure" find actualization. The genesis collective thus continues, moment by moment, amidst all its losses, to emerge.

> How manifold are your works! In wisdom you have made them all.
>
> —Ps. 104:24

Notes

1. For the full version of the argument of *creatio ex profundis*, including more detailed references, see Catherine Keller, *Face of the Deep: A Theology of Becoming* (London: Routledge, 2003).

2. Ibid., 114.

3. Michel Serres, *Genesis*, trans. Genevieve James and James Nielson (Ann Arbor: University of Michigan Press, 1995), 118.

4. Cf. Brian Green, *Elegant Universe: Superstrings, Hidden Dimensions, and the Quest for the Ultimate Theory* (New York: Norton, 99), 135.

5. Gerhard von Rad, drawing from Deut. 32:11 and Jer. 23:9, identifies "vibrate" as an apt translation of *mrhpht*; *Genesis: A Commentary*, rev. ed. (Philadelphia: Westminster, 1972), 49.

6. Cf. Jason Starr's documentary film, *What the Universe Tells Me: Unraveling the Mysteries of Mahler's Third Symphony* (Video Artists International, Inc., 2004). I happen to be one of its talking heads.

7. Karen Baker-Fletcher, *Sisters of Dust, Sisters of Spirit: Womanist Wordings on God and Creation* (Minneapolis: Fortress Press, 1998), 25.

8. Stuart A. Kauffman, *Investigations* (Oxford and New York: Oxford University Press, 2000), 119.

9. Julian of Norwich, *Showings*, trans. Edmund Colledge and James Walsh, preface by Jean Leclercq (New York: Paulist, 1978), Long Text, chap. 5 and chap. 8, 184, 190.

10. John Wesley's third sermon, "Upon Our Lord's Sermon on the Mount," quoted in John B. Cobb Jr., *Grace and Responsibility: A Wesleyan Theology for Today* (Nashville: Abingdon, 1995), 50.

11. For the major development of the metaphor of the universe as God's body, see Sallie McFague, *The Body of God: An Ecological Theology* (Minneapolis: Fortress Press, 1993). See a prior form in Charles Hartshorne, *Omnipotence and Other Theological Mistakes* (Albany: State University of New York, 1984); and a subsequent form in Catherine Keller, "The Flesh of God: A Metaphor in the Wild," in *Theology That Matters: Ecology, Economy, and God*, ed. Darby Kathleen Ray (Minneapolis: Fortress Press, 2006).

12. Bill Moyers, *Is God Green?*, www.pbs.org/moyers/moyers onamerica/green/.

13. Ibid.

14. Annie Dillard, *Pilgrim at Tinker Creek* (New York: Harper Perennial, 1985), 9.

15. Baker-Fletcher, *Sisters*, 25.

16. "In the beginning was the word. The word proselytised the sea with its message, copying itself unceasingly and forever. The word discovered how to rearrange chemicals so as to capture little

eddies in the stream of entropy and make them live. The word transformed the land surface of the planet from a dusty hell to a verdant paradise. The word eventually blossomed and became sufficiently ingenious to build a porridgy contraption called a human brain that could discover and be aware of the word itself"; Matt Ridley, *Genome: The Autobiography of a Species in 23 Chapters* (New York: HarperCollins, 1999), 11.

17. Genes, continues Ridley, "may direct the construction of the body and brain in the womb, but then they set about dismantling and rebuilding what they have made almost at once—in response to experience. They are both cause and consequence of our actions"; *Nature Via Nurture: Genes, Experience, & What Makes Us Human* (New York: HarperCollins, 2003), 6.

18. John the Scot (Joannes Scotus Eriugena), *Periphyseon = On the Division of Nature*, trans. Myra I. Uhlfelder and summaries by Jean A. Potter (Indianapolis: Bobbs-Merrill, 1976), 137.

19. See the Discovery Institute/Center for Science and Culture at www.discovery.org/csc/.

20. Ian G. Barbour, *When Science Meets Religion: Enemies, Strangers, or Partners?* (San Francisco: HarperSanFrancisco, 2000), 164.

Pierre Teilhard de Chardin, On Evolutionary Spirituality

Selections from *The Divine Milieu*

From Part One

The Divinisation of Our Activities

Note: It is of the utmost importance at this point to bear in mind what was said at the end of the Preface. We use the word "activity" in the ordinary, everyday sense, without in any way denying—far from it—all that occurs between *grace* and the *will* in the infra-experimental spheres of the soul. To repeat: what is most divine in God is that, in an absolute sense, we are nothing apart from him. The least admixture of what may be called Pelagianism would suffice to ruin immediately the beauties of the divine *milieu* in the eyes of the "seer."

Of the two halves or components into which our lives may be divided, the most important, judging by appearances and by the price we set upon it, is the sphere of activity, endeavour, and development. There can, of course, be no action without reaction. And, of course, there is nothing in us which in origin and at its deepest is not, as St. Augustine said, "*in nobis, sine nobis.*" When we act, as it seems, with the greatest spontaneity and vigour, we are to some extent led by the things we imagine we are controlling. Moreover, the very expansion of our energy (which reveals the core of our autonomous personality) is, ultimately, only our obedience to a will to be and to grow, of which we can master neither the varying intensity nor the countless modes. We shall return, at the beginning of Part Two, to these essentially passive elements, some of which form part of the very marrow of our being, while others are diffused among the inter-play of universal causes which we call our "character," our "nature," or our "good and bad luck." For the moment let us consider our life in terms of the categories and definitions which are the most immediate and universal. Everyone can distinguish quite clearly between the moments in which he is acting and those in which he is acted upon. Let us look at ourselves in one of those phases of dominant activity and try to see how, with the help of our activity and by developing it to the full, the divine presses in upon us and seeks to enter our lives.

1. The Undoubted Existence of the Fact and the Difficulty of Explaining It: The Christian Problem of the Sanctification of Action

Nothing is more certain, dogmatically, than that human action can be sanctified. "Whatever you do," says St. Paul, "do it in the name of our Lord Jesus Christ." And the dearest of Christian traditions has always been to interpret those words to mean: in intimate union with our Lord Jesus Christ. St. Paul himself, after calling upon us to "put on Christ," goes on to forge the famous series of words *collaborare, compati, commori, con-ressuscitare*, giving them the fullest possible meaning, a literal meaning even, and expressing the conviction that every human life must—in some sort—become a life in common with the life of Christ. The actions of life, of which Paul is speaking here, should not, as everyone knows, be understood solely in the sense of religious and devotional "works" (prayers, fastings, alms-givings). It is the whole of human life, down to its most "natural" zones, which, the Church teaches, can be sanctified. "Whether you eat or whether you drink,"

St. Paul says. The whole history of the Church is there to attest it. Taken as a whole, then, from the most solemn declarations or examples of the pontiffs and doctors of the Church to the advice humbly given by the priest in confession, the general influence and practice of the Church has always been to dignify, ennoble, and transfigure in God the duties inherent in one's station in life, the search for natural truth, and the development of human action.

The fact cannot be denied. But its legitimacy—that is. its logical coherence with the whole basis of the Christian temper—is not immediately evident. How is it that the perspectives opened up by the kingdom of God do not, by their very presence, shatter the distribution and balance of our activities? How can the man who believes in heaven and the Cross continue to believe seriously in the value of worldly occupations? How can the believer, in the name of everything that is most Christian in him, carry out his duty as man to the fullest extent and as whole-heartedly and freely as if he were on the direct road to God? That is what is not altogether clear at first sight; and in fact it disturbs more minds than one thinks.

The question might be put in this way:

According to the most sacred articles of his *Credo*, the Christian believes that life here below is continued in a life of which the joys, the sufferings, the reality, are quite incommensurable with the present conditions in our universe. This contrast and disproportion are enough, by themselves, to rob us of our taste for the world and our interest in it; but to them must be added a positive doctrine of judgment upon, even disdain for, a fallen and vitiated world. "Perfection consists in detachment; the world around us is vanity and ashes." The believer is constantly reading or hearing these austere words. How can he reconcile them with that other counsel, usually coming from the same master and in any case written in his heart by nature, that he must be an example unto the Gentiles in devotion to duty, in energy, and even in leadership in all the spheres opened up by man's activity? There is no need for us to consider the wayward or the lazy who cannot be bothered to acquire an understanding of their world, or seek with care to advance their fellows' welfare—from which they will benefit a hundredfold after their last breath—and only contribute to the human task "with the tips of their fingers." But there is a kind of human spirit (known to every spiritual director) for whom this difficulty assumes the shape and importance of a besetting and numbing uncertainty. Such spirits, set upon interior unity, become the victims of a veritable spiritual dualism. On the one hand a very sure instinct, mingled with their love for that which is and their taste for life, draws them to the joy of creating and of knowing. On the other hand, a higher will to love God above all else makes them afraid of the least division or deflection in their allegiances. In the most spiritual layers of their being they experience a tension between the opposing ebb and flow caused by the drawing power of the two rival stars we spoke of at the beginning: God and the world. Which of the two is to make itself more nobly adored?

Depending on the greater or lesser vitality of the nature of the individual, this conflict is in danger of finding its solution in one of the three following ways: either the Christian will repress his taste for the tangible and force himself to confine his concern to purely religious objects, and he will try to live in a world that he has divinised by banishing the largest possible number of earthly objects; or else, harassed by that inward conflict which hampers him, he will dismiss the evangelical counsels and decide to lead what seems to him a complete and human life; or else, again, and this is the most usual case, he will give up any attempt to make sense of his situation; he will never belong wholly to God, nor ever wholly to things; incomplete in his own eyes, and insincere in the eyes of his fellows, he will gradually acquiesce in a double life. I am speaking, it should not be forgotten, from experience.

For various reasons, all three of these solutions are to be feared. Whether we become distorted, disgusted, or divided, the result is equally bad, and certainly contrary to that which Christianity should rightly produce in us. There is, without possible doubt, a fourth way out of the problem: it consists in seeing how, without making the smallest concession to "nature" but with a thirst for greater perfection, we can reconcile, and provide mutual nourishment for, the love of God and the healthy love of the world, a striving toward detachment and a striving toward the enrichment of our human lives. . . .

Let us look at the two solutions that can be brought to the Christian problem of "the divinisation of human activity," the first partial, the second complete.

2. An Incomplete Solution: Human Action Has No Value Other Than the Intention Which Directs It

If we try somewhat crudely to reduce to its barest bones the immediate answer given by spiritual directors to those who ask them how a Christian, who is determined to disdain the world and jealously to keep his heart for God, can love what he is doing (his work)—in conformity with the Church's teaching that the faithful should take *not a lesser* but a *fuller* part than the pagan—it will run along these lines:

You are anxious, my friend, to restore its value to your human endeavour; to you the characteristic viewpoints of Christian asceticism seem to set far too little store by such activity. Very well then, you must let the clear spring water of purity of intention flow into your work, as if it were its very substance. Cleanse your intention, and the least of your actions will be filled with God. Certainly the material side of your actions has no definitive value. Whether men discover one truth or one fact more or less, whether or not they make beautiful music or beautiful pictures, whether their organisation of the world is more or less successful—all that has no direct importance for heaven. None of these discoveries or creations will become one of the stones of which is built the New Jerusalem. But what *will* count, up there, what *will* always endure, is this: that you have acted in all things *conformably* to the will of God.

God obviously has no need of the products of your busy activity, since he could give himself everything without you. The only thing that concerns him, the only thing he desires intensely, is your faithful use of your freedom, and the preference you accord him over the things around you.

Try to grasp this: the things which are given to you on earth are given you purely as an exercise, a "blank sheet" on which you make your own mind and heart. You are on a testing-ground where God can judge whether you are capable of being translated to heaven and into his presence. You are on trial. So that it matters very little what becomes of the fruits of the earth, or what they are worth. The whole question is whether you have used them in order to learn how to obey and how to love.

You should not, therefore, set store by the coarse outer-covering of your human actions: this can be burnt like straw or smashed like china. Think, rather, that into each of these humble vessels you can pour, like a sap or a precious liquor, the spirit of obedience and of union with God. If worldly aims have no value in themselves, you can love them for the opportunity they give you of proving your faithfulness to God.

We are not suggesting that the foregoing words have ever
been actually used; but we believe they convey a nuance which
is often discernible in spiritual direction, and we are sure
that they give a rough idea of what a good number of the
"directed" have understood and retained of the exhortations
given them.

On this assumption let us examine the attitude which they
recommend.

In the first place this attitude contains an enormous part
of truth. It is perfectly right to exalt the role of a good intention as the necessary start and foundation of all else; indeed—a
point which we shall have to make again—it is the golden
key which unlocks our inward personal world to God's presence. It expresses vigorously the primary worth of the divine
will which, by virtue of this attitude, becomes for the Christian
(as it was for his divine model) the fortifying marrow of all
earthly nourishment. It reveals a sort of unique *milieu*, un-
changing beneath the diversity and number of the tasks which,
as men and women, we have to do, in which we can place
ourselves without ever having to withdraw.

These various features convey a first and essential approx-
imation to the solution we are looking for; and we shall certainly retain them in their entirety in the more satisfactory plan
of the interior life which will soon be suggested. But they seem
to us to lack the achievement which our spiritual peace and
joy so imperiously demand. The divinisation of our endeavour
by the value of the intention put into it, pours a priceless *soul*
into all our actions; but *it does not confer the hope of resurrection upon their bodies*. Yet that hope is what we need if our
joy is to be complete. It is certainly a very great thing to be able
to think that, if we love God, something of our inner activity,
of our *operatio*, will never be lost. But will not the work itself
of our minds, of our hearts, and of our hands—that is to say,
our achievements, what we bring into being, our *opus*—will
not this, too, in some sense be "eternalized" and saved?

Indeed, Lord, it will be—by virtue of a claim which you yourself have implanted at the very centre of my will! I desire and need that it should be.

I desire it because I love irresistibly all that your continuous help enables me to bring each day to reality. A thought, a material improvement, a harmony, a unique nuance of human love, the enchanting complexity of a smile or a glance, all these new *beauties that appear for the first time, in me or around me, on the human face of the earth—I cherish them like children and cannot believe that they will die entirely in their flesh. If I believed that these things were to perish for ever, should I have given them life? The more I examine myself, the more I discover this psychological truth: that no one lifts his little finger to do the smallest task unless moved, however obscurely, by the conviction that he is contributing infinites- imally (at least indirectly) to the building of something defin- itive—that is to say, to your work, my God. This may well sound strange or exaggerated to those who act without thor- oughly scrutinising themselves. And yet it is a fundamental law of their action. It requires no less than the pull of what men call the Absolute, no less than you yourself, to set in motion the frail liberty which you have given us. And that being so, everything which diminishes my explicit faith in the heavenly value of the* results *of my endeavour, diminishes irremediably my power to act.*

Show all your faithful, Lord, in what a full and true sense "their work follows them" into your kingdom—opera se- quuntur illos. Otherwise they will become like those idle workmen who are not spurred by their task. And even if a sound human instinct prevails over their hesitancies or the sophisms of an incompletely enlightened religious practice, they will remain fundamentally divided and frustrated; and it will be said that the sons of heaven cannot compete on the human level, in conviction and hence on equal terms, with the children of the world.

3. The Final Solution: All Endeavour Cooperates to Complete the World in Christo Jesu

The general ordering of the salvation (which is to say the divinisation) of what we do can be expressed briefly in the following syllogism.

At the heart of our universe, each soul exists for God, in our Lord.

But all reality, even material reality, around each one of us, exists for our souls.

Hence, all sensible reality, around each one of us, exists, through our souls, for God in our Lord.

Let us examine each proposition of the syllogism in turn and separately. Its terms and the link between them are easy to grasp. But we must beware: it is one thing to have understood its words, and another to have penetrated the astonishing world whose inexhaustible riches are revealed by its calm and formal exactitude.

A. At the heart of our universe, each soul exists for God in our Lord

The major of the syllogism does no more than express the fundamental Catholic dogma which all other dogmas merely explain or define. It therefore requires no proof here; but it does need to be strictly understood by the intelligence. Each soul exists for God in our Lord. We should not be content to give this destination of our being in Christ a meaning too obviously modeled on the legal relationships which in our world link an object to its owner. Its nature is altogether more physical and deeper. Because the consummation of the world (what Paul calls the Pleroma) is a communion of persons (the communion of saints), our minds require that we should express the links within that communion by analogies drawn from society. Moreover, in order to avoid the perverse pan-theism and materialism which lie in wait for our thought whenever it applies to its mystical concepts the powerful but dangerous resources of analogies drawn from organic life, the majority of theologians (more cautious on this point than St. Paul) do not favour too realist an interpretation of the links which bind the limbs to the head in the Mystical Body. But there is no reason why caution should become timidity. If we want a full and vivid understanding of the teachings of the Church (which alone makes them beautiful and acceptable) on the value of human life and the promises or threats of the future life—then, without rejecting anything of the forces of freedom and of consciousness which form the natural endowment proper to the human soul, we must perceive the existence of links between us and the Incarnate Word no less precise than those which control, in the world, the affinities of the elements in the building up of "natural" wholes.

There is no point, here, in seeking a new name by which to designate the super-eminent nature of that dependence, where all that is most flexible in human combinations and all that is most intransigent in organic structures merge harmoniously in a moment of final incandescence. We will continue to call it by the name that has always been used: *mystical* union. Far from implying some idea of diminution, we use the term to mean the strengthening and purification of the reality and urgency contained in the most powerful interconnections revealed to us in every order of the physical and human world. On that path we can advance without fear of over-stepping the truth; for everyone in the Church of God is agreed upon the fact itself, if not upon its system-atic statement: by virtue of the powerful incarnation of the Word, our soul is wholly dedicated to Christ and centered upon him.

B. *"In our universe," we went on to say, "in which each soul exists for God, in our Lord, all that is sensible, in its turn, exists for the soul."*

In the form in which we have given it, the minor of our syllogism is tinged with a certain "finalist" doctrine which may shock those with a positivist cast of mind. Nevertheless, it does no more than express an incontrovertible natural fact—which is that our spiritual being is continually nourished by the countless energies of the perceptible world. Here, again, proof is unnecessary. But it is essential to see—to see things as they are and to see them really and intensely. We live at the centre of the network of cosmic influences as we live at the heart of the human crowd or among the myriads of stars, without, alas, being aware of their immensity. If we wish to live our humanity and our Christianity to the full, we must overcome that insensitivity which tends to conceal things from us in proportion as they are too close to us or too vast. It is worth while performing the salutary exercise which consists in starting with those elements of our conscious life in which our awareness of ourselves as persons is most fully developed, and moving out from these to consider the spread of our being. We shall be astonished at the extent and the intimacy of our relationship with the universe.

Where are the roots of our being? In the first place they plunge back and down into the unfathomable past. How great is the mystery of the first cells which were one day animated by the breath of our souls! How impossible to decipher the welding of successive influences in which we are forever incorporated! In each one of us, through matter, the whole history of the world is in part reflected. And however autonomous our soul, it is indebted to an inheritance worked upon from all sides—before ever it came into being—by the totality of the energies of the earth: it meets and rejoins life at a determined level. Then, hardly has it entered actively into the universe at that particular point than it feels, in its turn, besieged and penetrated by the flow of cosmic influences which have to be ordered and assimilated. Let us look around us: the waves come from all sides and from the farthest horizon. Through every cleft the world we perceive floods us with its riches—food for the body, nourishment for the eyes, harmony of sounds and fullness of the heart, unknown phenomena and new truths, all these treasures, all these stimuli, all these calls, coming to us from the four corners of the world, cross our consciousness at every moment. What is their role within us? What will their effect be, even if we welcome them passively or indistinctly, like bad workmen? They will merge into the most intimate life of our soul and either develop it or poison it. We only have to look at ourselves for one moment to realise this, and either feel delight or anxiety. If even the most humble and most material of our foods is capable of deeply influencing our most spiritual faculties, what can be said of the infinitely more penetrating energies conveyed to us by the music of tones, of notes, of words, of ideas? We have not, in us, a body which takes its nourishment independently of our soul. Everything that the body has admitted and has begun to transform must be transfigured by the soul in its turn. The soul does this, no doubt, in its own way and with its own dignity. But it cannot escape from this universal contact nor from that unremitting labour. And that is how the characteristic power of understanding and loving, which will form its immaterial individuality, is gradually perfected in it for its own good and at its own risk. We hardly know in what proportions and under what guise our natural faculties will pass over into the final act of the vision of God. But it can hardly be doubted that, with God's help, it is here below that we give ourselves the eyes and the heart which a final transfiguration will make the organs of a power of adoration, and of a capacity for beatification, particular to each individual man and woman among us.

The masters of the spiritual life incessantly repeat that God wants only souls. To give those words their true value,

we must not forget that the human soul, however independently created our philosophy represents it as being, is
inseparable, in its birth and in its growth, from the universe
into which it is born. In each soul, God loves and partly saves
the whole world which that soul sums up in an incommuni-
cable and particular way. But this summing-up, this welding,
are not given to us ready-made and complete with the first
awakening of consciousness. It is we who, through our own
activity, must industriously assemble the widely scattered
elements. The labour of seaweed as it concentrates in its tissues
the substances scattered, in infinitesimal quantities, throughout the vast layers of the ocean; the industry of bees as they
make honey from the juices broadcast in so many flowers—
these are but pale images of the ceaseless working-over that
all the forces of the universe undergo in us in order to reach
the level of spirit.

Thus every man, in the course of his life, must not only show
himself obedient and docile. By his fidelity he must *build*—
starting with the most natural territory of his own self—a work,
an *opus*, into which something enters from all the elements of
the earth. *He makes his own soul* throughout all his earthly
days; and at the same time he collaborates in another work, in
another *opus*, which infinitely transcends, while at the same
time it narrowly determines, the perspectives of his individual
achievement: the completing of the world. For in presenting
the Christian doctrine of salvation, it must not be forgotten
that the world, taken as a whole, that is to say, insofar as it
consists in a hierarchy of souls—which appear only successively,
develop only collectively, and will be completed only in union—
the world, too, undergoes a sort of vast "ontogenesis" (a vast
becoming what it is) in which the development of each soul,
assisted by the perceptible realities on which it depends, is
but a diminished harmonic. Beneath our efforts to put spiritual
form into our own lives, the world slowly accumulates, starting with the whole of matter, that which will make of it the
Heavenly Jerusalem or the New Earth.

C. We can now bring together the major and minor of our syllogism so as to grasp the link between them and the conclusion

If it is true, as we know from the Creed, that souls enter so intimately into Christ and God, and if it is true, as we know from the most general conclusions of psychoanalysis, that the perceptible enters vitally into the most spiritual zones of our souls—then we must also recognise that in the whole process which from first to last activates and directs the elements of the universe, *everything forms a single whole*. And we begin to see more distinctly the great sun of Christ the King, of Christ *amictus mundo*, of the universal Christ, rising over our interior world. Little by little, stage by stage, everything is finally linked to the supreme centre *in quo omnia constant*. The streams which flow from this centre operate not only within the higher reaches of the world, where human activities take place in a distinctively supernatural and meritorious form. In order to save and establish these sublime forces, the power of the Word Incarnate penetrates matter itself; it goes down into the deepest depths of the lower forces. And the Incarnation will be complete only when the part of chosen substance contained in every object—given spiritual import once in our souls and a second time with our souls in Jesus—shall have rejoined the final centre of its completion. *Quid est quod ascendit, nisi quod prius descendit, ut repleret omnia?*

It is through the collaboration which he stimulates in us that Christ, starting from *all* created things, is consummated and attains his plenitude. St. Paul himself tells us so. We may, perhaps, imagine that the creation was finished long ago. But that would be quite wrong. It continues still more magnificently, and at the highest levels of the world. *Omnis creatura adhuc ingemiscit et parturit*. And we serve to complete it, even by the humblest work of our hands. That is, ultimately, the meaning and value of our acts. Owing to the interrelation between matter, soul, and Christ, we bring part of the being which he desires back to God *in whatever we do*. With each one of our *works*, we labour—in individual separation, but no less really—to build the Pleroma; that is to say, we bring to Christ a little fulfillment.

4. Communion through Action

Each one of our works, by its more or less remote or direct effect upon the spiritual world, helps to make perfect Christ in his mystical totality. That is the fullest possible answer to the question: How can we, following the call of St. Paul, see God in all the active half of our lives? In fact, through the unceasing operation of the Incarnation, the divine so thoroughly permeates all our creaturely energies that, in order to meet it and lay hold on it, we could not find a more fitting setting than that of our action.

To begin with, in action I adhere to the creative power of God; I coincide with it; I become not only its instrument but its living extension. And as there is nothing more personal in a being than his will, I merge myself, in a sense, through my heart, with the very heart of God. This commerce is continuous because I am always acting; and at the same time, since I can never set a boundary to the perfection of my fidelity nor to the fervour of my intention, this commerce enables me to liken myself, ever more strictly and indefinitely, to God.

The soul does not pause to relish this communion, nor does it lose sight of the material end of its action; for it is wedded to a *creative* effort. The will to succeed, a certain passionate delight in the work to be done, forms an integral part of our creaturely fidelity. It follows that the very sincerity with which we desire and pursue success for God's sake reveals itself as a new factor—also without limits—in our being knit together with him who animates us. Originally we had fellowship with God in the simple common exercise of wills; but now we unite ourselves with him in the shared love of the end for which we are working; and the crowning marvel is that, with the possession of this end, we have the utter joy of discovering his presence once again.

All this follows directly from what was said a moment back on the relationship between natural and supernatural actions in the world. Any increase that I can bring upon myself or upon things is translated into some increase in my power to love and some progress in Christ's blessed hold upon the universe. Our work appears to us, in the main, as a way of earning our daily bread. But its essential virtue is on a higher level: through it we complete in ourselves the subject of the divine union; and through it again we somehow make to grow in stature the divine term of the one with whom we are united, our Lord Jesus Christ. Hence whatever our role as men may be, whether we are artists, workingmen, or scholars, we can, if we are Christians, speed toward the object of our work as though toward an opening on to the supreme fulfillment of our beings. Indeed, without exaggeration or excess in thought or expression—but simply by confronting the most fundamental truths of our faith and of experience—we are led to the following observation: God is inexhaustibly attainable in the *totality* of our action. And this prodigy of divinisation has nothing with which we dare to compare it except the subtle, gentle sweetness with which this actual change of shape is wrought; for it is achieved without disturbing at all (*non minuit, sed sacravit . . .*) the completeness and unity of man's endeavour.

5. The Christian Perfection of Human Endeavour

There was reason to fear, as we have said, that the introduction of Christian perspectives might seriously upset the ordering of human action; that the seeking after, and waiting for, the kingdom of heaven might deflect human activity from its natural tasks, or at least entirely eclipse any interest in them.

Now we see why this cannot and must not be so. The knitting together of God and the world has just taken place under our eyes in the domain of action. No, God does not deflect our gaze prematurely from the work he himself has given us, since he presents himself to us as attainable through that very work. Nor does he blot out, in his intense light, the detail of our earthly aims, since the closeness of our union with him is in fact determined by the exact fulfillment of the least of our tasks. We ought to accustom ourselves to this basic truth 'til we are steeped in it, until it becomes as familiar to us as the perception of shape or the reading of words. God, in all that is most living and incarnate in him, is not far away from us, altogether apart from the world we see, touch, hear, smell and taste about us. Rather he awaits us every instant in our action, in the work of the moment. There is a sense in which he is at the tip of my pen, my spade, my brush, my needle—of my heart and of my thought. By pressing the stroke, the line, or the stitch, on which I am engaged, to its ultimate natural finish, I shall lay hold of that last end toward which my innermost will tends. Like those formidable physical forces which man contrives to discipline so as to make them perform operations of prodigious delicacy, so the tremendous power of the divine attraction is focused on our frail desires and microscopic intents without breaking their point. It sur-animates; hence it neither disturbs anything nor stifles anything. It sur-animates; hence it introduces a higher principle of unity into our spiritual life, the specific effect of which is—depending upon the point of view one adopts—either to make man's endeavour holy, or to give the Christian life the full flavour of humanity.

A. The sanctification of human endeavour

I do not think I am exaggerating when I say that nine out of ten practising Christians feel that man's work is always at the level of a "spiritual encumbrance." In spite of the practice of right intentions and the day offered every morning to God, the general run of the faithful dimly feel that time spent at the office or the studio, in the fields or in the factory, is time taken away from prayer and adoration. It is impossible not to work—that is taken for granted. Then it is impossible, too, to aim at the deep religious life reserved for those who have the leisure to pray or preach all day long. A few moments of the day can be salvaged for God, yes, but the best hours are absorbed, or at any rate cheapened, by material cares. Under the sway of this feeling, large numbers of Catholics lead a double or crippled life in practice: they have to step out of their human dress so as to have faith in themselves as Christians— and inferior Christians at that.

What has been said above of the divine extensions and God-given demands of the mystical or universal Christ should be enough to demonstrate both the emptiness of these impressions and the validity of the thesis (so dear to Christianity) of sanctification through fulfilling the duties of our station. There are, of course, certain noble and cherished moments of the day—those when we pray or receive the sacraments. Were it not for these moments of more efficient or explicit commerce with God, the tide of the divine omnipresence, and our perception of it, would weaken until all that was best in our human endeavour, without being entirely lost to the world, would be for us emptied of God. But once we have jealously safeguarded our relation to God encountered, if I may dare use the expression, "in his pure state" (that is to say, in a state of being distinct from all the constituents of the world), there is no need to fear that the most trivial or the most absorbing of occupations should force us to depart from him. To repeat: by virtue of the Creation and, still more, of the Incarnation, *nothing* here below *is profane* for those who know how to see. On the contrary, everything is sacred to the men who can distinguish that portion of chosen being which is subject to Christ's drawing power in the process of consummation. Try, with God's help, to perceive the connection—even physical and natural—which binds your labour with the building of the kingdom of heaven; try to realise that heaven itself smiles upon you and, through your works, draws you to itself; then, as you leave church for the noisy streets, you will remain with only one feeling, that of continuing to immerse yourself in God. If your work is dull or exhausting, take refuge in the inexhaustible and becalming interest of progressing in the divine life. If your work enthralls you, then allow the spiritual impulse which matter communicates to you to enter into your taste for God whom you know better and desire more under the veil of his works. Never, at any time, "whether eating or drinking," consent to do anything without first of all realising its significance and constructive value *in Christo Jesu* and pursuing it with all your might. This is not simply a commonplace precept for salvation: it is the very path to sanctity for each man according to his state and calling. For what is sanctity in a creature if not to adhere to God with the maximum of his strength?—and what does that maximum adherence to God mean if not the fulfillment—in the world organised around Christ—of the exact function, be it lowly or eminent, to which that creature is destined both by natural endowment and by supernatural gift?

Within the Church we observe all sorts of groups whose members are vowed to the perfect practice of this or that particular virtue: mercy, detachment, the splendour of the liturgy, the missions, contemplation. Why should there not be men vowed to the task of exemplifying, by their lives, the general sanctification of human endeavour?—men whose common religious ideal would be to give a full and conscious explanation of the divine possibilities or demands which any worldly occupation implies—men, in a word, who would devote themselves, in the fields of thought, art, industry, commerce, and politics, etc., to carrying out in the sublime spirit these demands—the basic tasks which form the very bonework of human society? Around us the "natural" progress which nourishes the sanctity of each new age is all too often left to the children of the world—that is to say, to agnostics or the irreligious. Unconsciously or involuntarily such men collaborate in the kingdom of God and in the fulfillment of the elect: their efforts, going beyond or correcting their incomplete or bad intentions, are gathered in by him "whose energy subjects all things to itself." But that is no more than a second best, a temporary phase in the organisation of human activity. Right from the hands that knead the dough, to those that consecrate it, the great and universal Host should be prepared and handled in a spirit of *adoration*.

May the time come when men, having been awakened to a sense of the close bond linking all the movements of this world in the single, all-embracing work of the Incarnation, shall be unable to give themselves to any one of their tasks without illuminating it with the clear vision that their work—however elementary it may be—is received and put to good use by a Centre of the universe.

When that comes to pass, there will be little to separate life in the cloister from the life of the world. And only then will the action of the children of heaven (at the same time as the action of the children of the world) have attained the intended plenitude of its humanity.

B. *The humanisation of Christian endeavour*

The great objection brought against Christianity in our time, and the real source of the distrust which insulates entire blocks of humanity from the influence of the Church, have nothing to do with historical or theological difficulties. It is the suspicion that our religion makes its followers *inhuman*.

"Christianity," so some of the best of the Gentiles are inclined to think, "is bad or inferior because it does not lead its followers to levels of attainment beyond ordinary human powers; rather it withdraws them from the ordinary ways of humankind and sets them on other paths. It isolates them instead of merging them with the mass. Instead of harnessing them to the common task, it causes them to lose interest in it. Hence, far from raising them to a higher level, it diminishes them and makes them false to their nature. Moreover, don't they admit as much themselves? And if one of their religious, or one of their priests, should happen to devote his life to research in one of the so-called secular disciplines, he is very careful, as a rule, to point out that he is only lending himself for a time to serve a passing whim of scholarly fashion or even something ultimately of the stuff of illusion, and that simply in order to show that Christians are not, after all, the stupidest of men. When a Catholic works with us, we invariably get the impression that he is doing so in a spirit of condescension. He appears to be interested, but in fact, because of his religion, he simply does not believe in the human effort as such. His heart is not really with us. Christianity nourishes deserters and false friends: that is what we cannot forgive."

We have placed this objection, which would be deadly if it were true, in the mouth of an unbeliever. But has it no echo, here and there, within the most faithful souls? What Christian who has become aware of a sheet of glass insulating him from his nonbelieving colleagues has not asked himself uneasily whether he was not on a false tack or had not actually lost touch with the main current of mankind?

Without denying that some Christians, by their words more than their deeds, do give grounds for the reproach of being, if not the "enemies," at least the "stragglers" of the human race, we can safely assert, after what we said above concerning the supernatural value of our work on earth, that their attitude is due to an incomplete understanding and not at all to some ineradicable flaw in our religion.

How could we be deserters, or skeptical about the future of the tangible world? How could we be repelled by human labour? How little you know us! You suspect us of not sharing your concern and your hopes and your excitement as you penetrate the mysteries and conquer the forces of nature.

"Feelings of this kind," you say, "can only be shared by men struggling side by side for existence; whereas you Christians profess to be saved already." As though for us as for you, indeed far more than for you, it were not a matter of life and death that the earth should flourish to the uttermost of its natural powers. As far as you are concerned (and it is here that you are not yet human enough, you do not *go to the limits* of your humanity) it is simply a matter of the success or failure of a reality which remains vague and precarious even when conceived in the form of some super-humanity. For us it is a question in a true sense of achieving the victory of no less than a God. One thing is infinitely disappointing, I grant you: far too many Christians are insufficiently conscious of the "divine" responsibilities of their lives, and live like other men, giving only half of themselves, never experiencing the spur or the intoxication of advancing God's kingdom in every domain of mankind. But do not blame anything but our weakness: our faith imposes on us the right and the duty to throw ourselves into the things of the earth. As much as you, and even better than you (because, of the two of us, I alone am in a position to prolong the perspectives of my endeavour to infinity, in conformity with the requirements of my present intention), I want to dedicate myself body and soul to the sacred duty of research. We must test every barrier, try every path, plumb every abyss. *Nihil intentatum* . . . God wills it, who willed that he should have need of it. You are men, you say? *Plus et ego.*

Plus et ego. There can be no doubt of it. At a time when the consciousness of its own powers and possibilities is legitimately awakening in a mankind now ready to become adult, one of the first duties of a Christian as an apologist is to show, by the logic of his religious views and still more by the logic of his action, that the incarnate God did not come to diminish in us the glorious responsibility and splendid ambition that is ours: *of fashioning our own self*. Once again, *non minuit, sed sacravit*. No, Christianity is not, as it is sometimes presented and sometimes practised, an additional burden of observances and obligations to weigh down and increase the already heavy load, or to multiply the already paralysing ties of our life in society. It is, in fact, a soul of immense power which bestows significance and beauty and a new lightness on what we are already doing. It is true that it sets us on the road toward unsuspected heights. But the slope which leads to these heights is linked so closely with the one we were already climbing naturally, that there is nothing so distinctively human in the Christian (and this is what remains to be considered) as his detachment.

6. Detachment through Action

There hardly seems room for any dispute between Christians about what we have so far said about the *intrinsic* divinisation of human endeavour, since we have confined ourselves, in establishing it, to taking, in their proper strict sense, certain universally recognised theoretical and practical truths and confronting them with each other.

Nevertheless, some readers, though without finding any specific flaw in our argument, may feel vaguely upset or uneasy in the face of a Christian ideal which lays such stress on the preoccupations of human development and the pursuit of earthly improvements. They should bear in mind that we are still only halfway along the road which leads to the mountain of the Transfiguration. Up to this point we have been dealing only with the active part of our lives. In a moment or two, when we come to the chapter on passivities and diminishment, the arms of the Cross will begin to dominate the scene more widely. Let us consider it for a moment. In the very optimistic and very broadening attitude which has been roughly sketched above, a true and deep renunciation lies concealed. Anyone who devotes himself to human duty according to the Christian formula, though outwardly he may seem to be immersed in

the concerns of the earth, is in fact, down to the depths of his
being, a man of great detachment.

Of its very nature work is a manifold instrument of detachment, provided a man gives himself to it faithfully and
without rebellion. In the first place it implies effort and a
victory over inertia. And then, however interesting and intellectual it may be (and the more intellectual it is, the truer this
becomes), work is always accompanied by the painful pangs
of birth. Men can only escape the terrible boredom of mo-
notonous and commonplace duty to find themselves a prey
to the inner tension and the anxieties of "creation." To create
or organise material energy, or truth, or beauty brings with
it an inner torment which prevents those who face its hazards
from sinking into the quiet and closed-in life wherein grows
the vice of self-regard and attachment (in the technical sense).
An honest workman not only surrenders his calm and peace
once and for all but must learn continually to jettison the
form which his labour or art or thought first took and go in
search of new forms. To pause, so as to bask in or possess
results, would be a betrayal of action. Over and over again
he must go beyond himself, tear himself away from himself,
leaving behind him his most cherished beginnings. And on
that road, which is not so different from the royal road of the
Cross as might appear at first sight, detachment does not
consist only in continually replacing one object with another
of the same order—as miles, on a flat road, replace miles. By
virtue of a marvelous mounting force contained in things (and
which will be analysed in greater detail when we consider the
"spiritual power of matter"), each reality attained and left
behind gives us access to the discovery and pursuit of an ideal
of higher spiritual content. Those who spread their sails in
the right way to the winds of the earth will always find themselves borne by a current toward the open seas. The more
nobly a man wills and acts, the more avid he becomes for
great and sublime aims to pursue. He will no longer be content
with family, country and the remunerative aspect of his work.

He will want wider organisations to create, new paths to blaze, causes to uphold, truths to discover, an ideal to cherish and defend. So, gradually, the worker no longer belongs to himself. Little by little the great breath of the universe has insinuated itself into him through the fissure of his humble but faithful action, has broadened him, raised him up, borne him on.

It is in the Christian, provided he knows how to make the most of the resources of his faith, that these effects will reach their climax and their crown. As we have seen, from the point of view of the reality, accuracy and splendour of the ultimate end toward which we must aim in the least of our acts, we, disciples of Christ, are the most favoured of men. The Christian knows that his function is to divinise the world in Jesus Christ. In him, therefore, the natural process which drives human action from ideal to ideal and toward objects ever more internally coherent and comprehensive in their embrace, reaches—thanks to the support of Revelation—its fullest expansion. And in him, consequently, detachment through action should produce its maximum effectiveness.

And this is perfectly true. The Christian as we have described him in these pages is at once the most attached and the most detached of men. Convinced in a way in which the "worldly" cannot be of the unfathomable importance and value concealed beneath the humblest worldly successes, the Christian is at the same time as convinced as the hermit of the worthlessness of any success which is envisaged only as a benefit to himself (or even a general one) without reference to God. It is God and God alone whom he pursues through the reality of created things. For him, interest lies truly *in* things, but in absolute dependence upon God's presence in them. The light of heaven becomes perceptible and attainable to him in the crystalline transparency of beings. But he wants only this light, and if the light is extinguished, whether because the object is out of its true place, or has outlived its function, or has moved itself, then even the most precious substance is only ashes in his sight. Similarly, within himself and his most personal development, it is not himself that he is seeking, but that which is greater than he, to which he knows that he is destined. In his own view he himself no longer counts, no longer exists; he has forgotten and lost himself in the very endeavour which is making him perfect. It is no longer the atom which lives, but the universe within it.

Not only has he encountered God in the entire field of his actions in the perceptible world, but in the course of this first phase of his spiritual development, the divine *milieu* which has been uncovered absorbs his powers in the very proportion in which these laboriously rise above their individuality.

From Part Two

The Divinisation of Our Passivities

While man by the very development of his powers is led to discover ever vaster and higher aims for his action, he also tends to be dominated by the object of his conquests and, like Jacob wrestling with the Angel, he ends by adoring what he was struggling against. The scale of that which he has unveiled and unleashed brings him into subjection. And then, because of his nature as element, he is brought to recognise that, in the final act that is to unite him to the All, the two terms of the union are utterly disproportionate. He, the lesser, has to receive rather than to give. He finds himself in the grip of what he thought he could grasp.

The Christian, who is by right the first and most human of men, is more subject than others to this psychological reversal whereby, in the case of all intelligent creatures, joy in action imperceptibly melts into desire for submission, and the exaltation of becoming one's own self into the zeal to die in another. Having been perhaps primarily alive to the attractions of union with God through action, he begins to conceive and then to desire a complementary aspect, an ulterior phase, in his communion: one in which he would not develop himself so much as lose himself in God.

He does not have to look far to discover possibilities and opportunities for fulfillment in this gift of self. They are offered him at every moment—indeed they besiege him on all sides in the length and depth of the countless servitudes which make us servants far more than masters of the universe.

The moment has come to examine the number, the nature, and the possible divinisation of our passivities.

1. The Extent, Depth, and Diverse Forms of Human Passivities

The passivities of our lives, as we said at the beginning of this study, form half of human existence. The term means, quite simply, that that which is not done by us, is, by definition, undergone.

But this does not in any way prejudge the proportions in which action and passion possess our inner realm. In fact, these two parts of our lives—the active and the passive—are extraordinarily unequal. Seen from our point of view, the active occupies first place because we prefer it and because it is more easily perceived. But in the reality of things the passive is immeasurably the wider and the deeper part.

In the first place the passivities ceaselessly accompany our conscious deeds in the form of reactions which direct, sustain, or oppose our efforts. On this ground alone they inevitably and precisely coincide with the scope of our activities. But their sphere of influence extends far beyond these narrow limits. If we consider the matter carefully, we in fact perceive with a sort of dismay that it is only the fine point of ourselves that comes up into the light of self-consciousness and freedom. We know ourselves and set our own course but within an incredibly small radius of light. Immediately beyond lies impenetrable darkness, though it is full of presences—the night of everything that is within us and around us, without us and in spite of us. In this darkness, as vast, rich, troubled, and complex as the past and the present of the universe, we are not inert; we react, because we undergo. But this reaction, which operates without our control by an unknown prolongation of our being, is, humanly speaking, still a part of *our* passivity. In fact, everything beyond a certain distance is dark, and yet everything is full of being around us. This is the darkness, heavy with promises and threats, which the Christian will have to illuminate and animate with the divine presence.

In the midst of the confused energies which people this restless night, our mere presence immediately brings about the formation of two groups which press in upon us and demand to be treated in very different ways. On one side, the friendly and favourable forces, those which uphold our endeavour and point the way to success—the "passivities of growth." On the other side, the hostile powers which laboriously obstruct our tendencies, hamper or deflect our progress toward heightened being, and thwart our real or apparent capacities for development: these are the "passivities of diminishment."

Let us look at each group in turn; let us look them in the face until, in the depth of their alluring, unrevealing, or hostile gaze, we discern the kindling light of the blessed countenance of God.

2. The Passivities of Growth and the Two Hands of God

Growth seems so natural to us that we do not, as a matter of fact, pause to separate from our action the forces which nourish that action or the circumstances which favour its success. And yet, *quid habes quod non accepisti* (what dost thou possess that thou hast not previously received)? We undergo life as much as we undergo death, if not more.

We must try to penetrate our most secret self and examine our being from all sides. Let us try, patiently, to perceive the ocean of forces to which we are subjected and in which our growth is, as it were, steeped. This is a salutary exercise; for the depth and universality of our dependence on so much altogether outside our control all go to make up the embracing intimacy of our communion with the world to which we belong.

. . . And so, for the first time in my life perhaps (although I am supposed to meditate every day!), I took the lamp and, leaving the zone of everyday occupations and relationships where everything seems clear, I went down into my inmost self, to the deep abyss whence I feel dimly that my power of action emanates. But as I moved further and further away from the conventional certainties by which social life is superficially illuminated, I became aware that I was losing contact with myself. At each step of the descent a new person was disclosed within me of whose name I was no longer sure, and who no longer obeyed me. And when I had to stop my exploration because the path faded from beneath my steps, I found a bottomless abyss at my feet, and out of it came— arising I know not from where—the current which I dare to call *my* life.

What science will ever be able to reveal to man the origin, nature, and character of that conscious power to will and to love which constitutes his life? It is certainly not our effort, nor the effort of anyone around us, which set that current in motion. And it is certainly not our anxious care, nor that of any friend of ours, which prevents its ebb or controls its turbulence. We can, of course, trace back through generations some of the antecedents of the torrent which bears us along; and we can, by means of certain moral and physical disciplines and stimulants, regularise or enlarge the aperture through which the torrent is released into us. But neither that geography nor those artifices help us in theory or in practice to harness the sources of life. My self is given to me far more than it is formed by me. Man, Scripture says, cannot add a cubit to his stature. Still less can he add a unit to the potential of his love or accelerate by another unit the fundamental rhythm which regulates the ripening of his mind and heart. In the last resort the profound life, the fontal life, the newborn life, escape our grasp entirely.

Stirred by my discovery, I then wanted to return to the light of day and forget the disturbing enigma in the comfortable surroundings of familiar things—to begin living again at the surface without imprudently plumbing the depths of the abyss. But then, beneath this very spectacle of the turmoil of life, there reappeared, before my newly opened eyes, the unknown that I wanted to escape. This time it was not hiding at the bottom of an abyss; it disguised its presence in the innumerable strands which form the web of chance, the very stuff of which the universe and my own small individuality are woven. Yet it was the same mystery without a doubt: I recognised it. Our mind is disturbed when we try to plumb the depth of the world beneath us. But it reels still more when we try to number the favourable chances which must coincide at every moment if the least of living things is to survive and to succeed in its enterprises. After the consciousness of being something other and something greater than myself—a second thing made me dizzy: namely, the supreme improbability, the tremendous unlikelihood of finding myself existing in the heart of a world that has survived and succeeded in being a world.

At that moment, as anyone else will find who cares to make this same interior experiment, I felt the distress characteristic to a particle adrift in the universe, the distress which makes human wills founder daily under the crushing number of living things and of stars. And if something saved me, it was hearing the voice of the Gospel, guaranteed by divine successes, speaking to me from the depth of the night: *ego sum, noli timere* (It is I, be not afraid).

Yes, O God, I believe it: and I believe it all the more willingly because it is not only a question of my being consoled,

*but of my being completed: it is you who are at the origin of
the impulse, and at the end of that continuing pull which all
my life long I can do no other than follow, or favour the first
impulse and its developments. And it is you who vivify, for
me, with your omnipresence (even more than my spirit vivifies
the matter which it animates), the myriad influences of which
I am the constant object. In the life which wells up in me and
in the matter which sustains me, I find much more than your
gifts. It is you yourself whom I find, you who makes me participate in your being, you who moulds me. Truly in the ruling
and in the first disciplining of my living strength, in the continually beneficent play of secondary causes, I touch, as near
as possible, the two faces of your creative action, and I encounter, and kiss, your two marvelous hands—the one which
holds us so firmly that it is merged, in us, with the sources of
life, and the other whose embrace is so wide that, at its slightest
pressure, all the springs of the universe respond harmoniously
together. By their very nature, these blessed passivities which
are, for me, the will to be, the wish to be thus and thus, and
the chance of fulfilling myself according to my desire, are all
charged with your influence—an influence which will shortly
appear more distinctly to me as the organising energy of the
mystical body. In order to communicate with you in them in
a fontal communion (a communion in the sources of Life), I
have only to recognise you in them, and to ask you to be ever
more present in them.*

*O God, whose call precedes the very first of our movements,
grant me the desire to desire being—that, by means of that
divine thirst which is your gift, the access to the great waters
may open wide within me. Do not deprive me of the sacred
taste for being, that primordial energy, that very first of our
points of rest: Spiritu principali confirma me. And you whose
loving wisdom forms me out of all the forces and all the
hazards of the earth, grant that I may begin to sketch the
outline of a gesture whose full power will only be revealed to
me in presence of the forces of diminishment and death; grant*

that, after having desired, I may believe, and believe ardently and above all things, in your active presence.

Thanks to you, that expectation and that faith are already full of operative virtue. But how am I to set about showing you and proving to myself, through some external effort, that I am not one of those who say Lord, Lord! with their lips only? I shall work together with your action which ever forestalls me and will do so doubly. First, to your deep inspiration which commands me to be, I shall respond by taking great care never to stifle nor distort nor waste my power to love and to do. Next, to your all-embracing providence which shows me at each moment, by the day's events, the next step to take and the next rung to climb, I shall respond by my care never to miss an opportunity of rising "toward the level of spirit."

The life of each one of us is, as it were, woven of those two threads: the thread of inward development, through which our ideas and affections and our human and religious attitudes are gradually formed; and the thread of outward success by which we always find ourselves at the exact point where the whole sum of the forces of the universe meet together to work in us the effect which God desires.

O God, that at all times you may find me as you desire me and where you would have me be, that you may lay hold on me fully, both by the Within and the Without of myself, grant that I may never break this double thread of my life.

3. The Passivities of Diminishment[1]

To cleave to God hidden beneath the inward and outward forces which animate our being and sustain it in its development, is ultimately to open ourselves to, and put trust in, all the breaths of life. We answer to, and "communicate" with, the passivities of growth by our fidelity in action. Hence by our very desire to experience God passively we find ourselves brought back to the lovable duty of growth.

The moment has come to plumb the decidedly negative side of our existences—the side on which, however far we search, we cannot discern any happy result or any solid conclusion to what happens to us. It is easy enough to understand that God can be grasped in and through every life. But can God also be found in and through every death? This is what perplexes us deeply. And yet this is what we must learn to acknowledge as a matter of settled habit and practice, unless we abandon all that is most characteristically Christian in the Christian outlook; and unless we are prepared to forfeit commerce with God in one of the most widespread and at the same time most profoundly passive and receptive experiences of human life.

The forces of diminishment are our real passivities. Their number is vast, their forms infinitely varied, their influence constant. In order to clarify our ideas and direct our meditation we will divide them into two groups corresponding to the two forms under which we considered the forces of growth: the diminishments whose origin lies *within us*, and the diminishments whose origin lies *outside us*.

The external passivities of diminishment are all our bits of ill fortune. We have only to look back on our lives to see them springing up on all sides: the barrier which blocks our way, the wall that hems us in, the stone which throws us from our path, the obstacle that breaks us, the invisible microbe that kills the body, the little word that infects the mind, all the incidents and accidents of varying importance and varying kinds, the tragic interferences (upsets, shocks, severances, deaths) which come between the world of "other" things and the world that radiates out from us. And yet when hail, fire, and thieves had taken everything from Job—all his wealth and all his family—Satan could say to God, "Skin for skin, and all that a man hath he will give for his life. But put forth thy hand, and touch his bone and his flesh: and then thou shalt see that he will bless thee to thy face." In a sense the loss of things means little to us because we can always imagine getting them back. What is terrible for us is to be cut off from things through some inward diminishment that can never be retrieved.

Humanly speaking, the internal passivities of diminishment form the darkest element and the most despairingly useless years of our life. Some were waiting to pounce on us as we first awoke: natural failings, physical defects, intellectual or moral weaknesses, as a result of which the field of our activities, of our enjoyment, of our vision, has been pitilessly limited since birth. Others were lying in wait for us later on and appeared as suddenly and brutally as an accident, or as stealthily as an illness. All of us one day or another will come to realise, if we have not already done so, that one or other of these sources of disintegration has lodged itself in the very heart of our lives. Sometimes it is the cells of the body that rebel or become diseased; at other times the very elements of our personality seem to be in conflict or to detach themselves from any sort of order. And then we impotently stand by and watch collapse, rebellion, and inner tyranny, and no friendly influence can come to our help. And if by chance we escape, to a greater or lesser extent, the critical forms of these assaults from without which appear deep within us and irresistibly destroy the strength, the light, and the love by which we live, there still remains that slow, essential deterioration which we cannot escape: old age little by little robbing us of ourselves and pushing us on toward the end. Time, which postpones possession, time which tears us away from enjoyment, time which condemns us all to death—what a formidable passivity is the passage of time. . . .

In death, as in an ocean, all our slow or swift diminishments flow out and merge. Death is the sum and consummation of all our diminishments: it is *evil* itself—purely physical evil, insofar as it results organically in the manifold structure of that physical nature in which we are immersed—but a moral evil too, insofar as in the society to which we belong, or in ourselves, the wrong use of our freedom, by spreading disorder, converts this manifold complexity of our nature into the source of all evil and all corruption.

We must overcome death by finding God in it. And by the same token, we shall find the divine established in our innermost hearts, in the last stronghold which might have seemed able to escape his reach.

Here again, as in the case of the "divinization" of our human activities, we shall find the Christian faith absolutely explicit in what it claims to be the case, and what it bids us do. Christ has conquered death, not only by suppressing its evil effects, but by reversing its sting. By virtue of Christ's rising again, nothing any longer kills inevitably but everything is capable of becoming the blessed touch of the divine hands, the blessed influence of the will of God upon our lives. However marred by our faults, or however desperate in its circumstances, our position may be, we can, by a total reordering, completely correct the world that surrounds us, and resume our lives in a favourable sense. *Diligentibus Deum omnia convertuntur in bonum.* That is the fact which dominates all explanation and all discussion.

But here again, as in the matter of the saving value of our human endeavour, our mind wants to validate to itself its hopes so as to surrender to them more completely.

Quomodo fiet istud? This study is all the more necessary because the Christian attitude to evil lends itself to some very dangerous misunderstandings. A false interpretation of Christian resignation, together with a false idea of Christian detachment, is the principal source of the antagonisms which make a great many Gentiles so sincerely hate the Gospel.

Let us ask ourselves how, and in what circumstances, our apparent deaths, that is to say the waste-matter of our existences, can find their necessary place in the establishment, around us, of the kingdom of God and the *milieu* of God. It will help us to do this if we thoughtfully distinguish two phases, two periods, in the process which culminates in the transfiguration of our diminishments. The first of these phases

is that of our struggle against evil. The second is that of defeat
and of its transfiguration.

A. *Our struggle with God against evil*

When a Christian suffers, he says, "God has touched me."
The words are preeminently true, though their simplicity
summarises a very complex series of spiritual operations; and
it is *only when we have gone right through that whole series
of operations* that we have the right to speak those words. For
if, in the course of our encounters with evil, we try to distinguish what the Schoolmen term "the instants of nature," we
shall have, on the contrary, to begin by saying "God wants
to free me from this diminishment—God wants me to help
him to take this cup from me." To struggle against evil and
to reduce to a minimum even the ordinary physical evil which
threatens us is unquestionably the first act of our Father who
is in heaven; it would be impossible to conceive him in any
other way, and still more impossible to love him.

It is a perfectly correct view of things—and strictly conso-
nant with the Gospel—to regard Providence across the ages
as brooding over the world in ceaseless effort to spare that
world its bitter wounds and to bind up its hurts. Most certainly it is God himself who, in the course of the centuries,
awakens the great benefactors of humankind, and the great
physicians, in ways that agree with the general rhythm of
progress. He it is who inspires, even among those furthest
from acknowledging his existence, the quest for every means
of comfort and every means of healing. Do not men acknowledge by instinct this divine presence when hatreds are quenched
and their protesting uncertainty resolved as they kneel to
thank each one of those who have helped their body or their
mind to freedom? Can there be any doubt of it? At the first
approach of the diminishments we cannot hope to find God
except by loathing what is coming upon us and doing our

best to avoid it. The more we repel suffering at that moment, with our whole heart and our whole strength,[2] the more closely we cleave to the heart and action of God.

B. *Our apparent failure and its transfiguration*

With God as our ally we are always certain of saving our souls. But we know too well that there is no guarantee that we shall always avoid suffering or even those inward defeats on account of which we can imagine our lives to ourselves as failures. In any event, all of us are growing old and all of us will die. This means to say that, however fine our resistance, at some moment or other we feel the constraining grip of the forces of diminishment against which we were fighting, gradually gaining mastery over the forces of life, and dragging us, physically vanquished, to the ground. But how can we be defeated if God is fighting on our side? or what does this defeat mean?

The problem of evil—that is to say, the reconciling of our failures, even the purely physical ones, with creative goodness and creative power—will always remain one of the most disturbing mysteries of the universe for both our hearts and our minds. A full understanding of the suffering of God's creatures (like that of the pains of the damned) presupposes in us an appreciation of the nature and value of "participated being" which, for lack of any point of comparison, we cannot have. Yet this much we can see: on the one hand, the work which God has undertaken in uniting himself intimately to created beings presupposes in them a slow preparation in the course of which they (*who already exist, but are not yet complete*) cannot of their nature avoid the risks (increased by an original fault) involved in the imperfect ordering of the manifold, in them and around them; and on the other hand, because the final victory of good over evil can only be completed in the *total* organisation of the world, our infinitely short individual lives could not hope to know the joy, here below, of entry into the Promised Land. We are like soldiers who fall during the assault which leads to peace. God does not therefore suffer a preliminary defeat in our defeat because, although we appear to succumb individually, the world, in which we shall live again, triumphs in and through our deaths.

But this first aspect of his victory, which is enough to assure us of his omnipotence, is made complete by another disclosure—perhaps more direct and in every case more immediately experienceable by each of us—of his universal authority. In virtue of his very perfections,[3] God cannot ordain that the elements of a world in the course of growth—or at least of a fallen world in the process of rising again—should avoid shocks and diminishments, even moral ones: *necessarium est ut scandala eveniant*. But God will make it good—he will take his revenge, if one may use the expression—by making evil itself serve a higher good of his faithful, the very evil which the present state of creation does not allow him to suppress immediately. Like an artist who is able to make use of a fault or an impurity in the stone he is sculpting or the bronze he is casting so as to produce more exquisite lines or a more beautiful tone, God, without sparing us the partial deaths, nor the final death, which form an essential part of our lives, transfigures them by integrating them in a better plan—*provided we lovingly trust in him*. Not only our unavoidable ills but our faults, even our most deliberate ones, can be embraced in that transformation, provided always we repent of them. Not everything is immediately good to those who seek God; but everything is capable of becoming good: *omnia convertuntur in bonum*.

What is the process and what are the phases by which God accomplishes this marvelous transformation of our deaths into a better life? Drawing on analogies from what we know how to bring about ourselves and reflecting on the constant attitude and practical teaching of the Church with regard to human suffering, we may perhaps hazard an answer to this question.

It could be said that Providence, for those who believe in it, converts evil into good in three principal ways. Sometimes the check we have undergone will divert our activity on to objects or toward a framework that are more propitious— though still situated on the level of the human ends we are pursuing. That is what happened with Job, whose final happiness was greater than his first. At other times, more often perhaps, the loss which afflicts us will oblige us to turn for the satisfaction of our frustrated desires to less material fields, which neither worm nor rust can corrupt. The lives of the saints and, generally speaking, the lives of all those who have been outstanding for intelligence or goodness, are full of these instances in which one can see the man emerging ennobled, tempered, and renewed from some ordeal, or even some downfall, which seemed bound to diminish or lay him low forever. Failure in that case plays for us the part that the elevator plays for an aircraft or the pruning knife for a plant. It canalises the sap of our inward life, disengages the purest "components" of our being in such a way as to make us shoot up higher and straighter. The collapse, even when a moral one, is thus transformed into a success which, however spiritual it may be is, nevertheless, felt *experimentally*. In the presence of St. Augustine, St. Mary Magdalen, or St. Lydwine, no one hesitates to think *felix dolor* or *felix culpa*. With the result that, up to this point, we still "understand" Providence.

But there are more difficult cases (the most common ones, in fact) where human wisdom is altogether out of its depth. At every moment we see diminishment, both in us and around us, which does not seem to be compensated by advantages on any perceptible plane: premature deaths, stupid accidents, weaknesses affecting the highest reaches of our being. Under blows such as these, man does not move upward in any direction that we can perceive; he disappears or remains grievously diminished. How can these diminishments which are altogether without compensation, wherein we see death at its most deathly, become for us a good? This is where we can see the third way in which Providence operates in the domain of our diminishments—the most effective way and the way which most surely makes us holy.

God, as we have seen, has already transfigured our sufferings by making them serve our conscious fulfillment. In his hands the forces of diminishment have perceptibly become the tool that cuts, carves, and polishes within us the stone which is destined to occupy a definite place in the heavenly Jerusalem. But he will do still more, for, as a result of his omnipotence impinging upon our faith, events which show themselves experimentally in our lives as pure loss will become an immediate factor in the union we dream of establishing with him.

Uniting oneself means, in every case, migrating, and dying partially in what one loves. But if, as we are sure, this being reduced to nothing in the other must be all the more complete the more we give our attachment to one who is greater than ourselves, then we can set no limits to the tearing up of roots that is involved on our journey into God. The progressive breaking-down of our self-regard by the "automatic" broadening of our human perspectives (analysed earlier), when accompanied by the gradual spiritualisation of our tastes and aspirations under the impact of certain setbacks, is no doubt a very real foretaste of that leap out of ourselves which must in the end deliver us from the bondage of ourselves into the service of the divine sovereignty. Yet the effect of this initial detachment is for the moment only to develop the centre of our personality to its utmost limits. Arrived at that ultimate point we may still have the impression of possessing ourselves in a supreme degree—of being freer and more active than ever. We have not yet crossed the critical point of our ex-centration, of our reversion to God. There is a further step to take: the one that makes us *lose all foothold within our-selves—oportet ilium crescere, me autem minui.* We are still not lost to ourselves. What will be the agent of that definitive transformation? Nothing else than death.

In itself, death is an incurable weakness of corporeal beings, complicated, in our world, by the influence of an original fall. It is the sum and type of all the forces that diminish us, and against which we must fight without being able to hope for a personal, direct, and immediate victory. Now the great victory of the Creator and Redeemer, in the Christian vision, is to have transformed what is in itself a universal power of diminishment and extinction into an essentially life-giving factor. God must, in some way or other, make room for himself, hollowing us out and emptying us, if he is finally to penetrate into us. And in order to assimilate us in him, he must break the molecules of our being so as to recast and remodel us. The function of death is to provide the necessary entrance into our inmost selves. It will make us undergo the required dissociation. It will put us into the state organically needed if the divine fire is to descend upon us. And in that way its fatal power to decompose and dissolve will be harnessed to the most sublime operations of life. What was by nature empty and void, a return to bits and pieces, can, in any human existence, become fullness and unity in God.

C. Communion through diminishment

It was a joy to me, O God, in the midst of the struggle, to feel that in developing myself I was increasing the hold that you have upon me; it was a joy to me, too, under the inward thrust of life or amid the favourable play of events, to abandon myself to your providence. Now that I have found the joy of utilising all forms of growth to make you, or to let you, grow in me, grant that I may willingly consent to this last phase of communion in the course of which I shall possess you by diminishing in you.

After having perceived you as he who is "a greater myself," grant, *when my hour comes, that I may recognise you under the species of each alien or hostile force that seems bent upon*

destroying or uprooting me. When the signs of age begin to
mark my body (and still more when they touch my mind);
when the ill that is to diminish me or carry me off strikes from
without or is born within me; when the painful moment comes
in which I suddenly awaken to the fact that I am ill or growing
old; and above all at that last moment when I feel I am losing
hold of myself and am absolutely passive within the hands of
the great unknown forces that have formed me; in all those
dark moments, O God, grant that I may understand that it
is you (provided only my faith is strong enough) who are
painfully parting the fibres of my being in order to penetrate
to the very marrow of my substance and bear me away within
yourself.

The more deeply and incurably the evil is encrusted in my
flesh, the more it will be you that I am harbouring—you as
a loving, active principle of purification and detachment. The
more the future opens before me like some dizzy abyss or
dark tunnel, the more confident I may be—if I venture for-
ward on the strength of your word—of losing myself and
surrendering myself in you, of being assimilated by your body,
Jesus.

You are the irresistible and vivifying force, O Lord, and
because yours is the energy, because, of the two of us, you are
infinitely the stronger, it is on you that falls the part of con-
suming me in the union that should weld us together. Vouch-
safe, therefore, something more precious still than the grace
for which all the faithful pray. It is not enough that I should
die while communicating. Teach me to treat my death as an
act of communion.

D. *True resignation*

The above analysis (in which we have tried to distinguish the
phases by which our diminishments may be divinised) has
helped us to *validate to ourselves* the Christian formula, which

is so comforting to those who suffer, "God has touched me. God has taken away from me. His will be done." As a result of this analysis we have understood how the two hands of God can reappear, more active and more penetrating than ever, beneath the evils that corrupt us from within, and the blows that break us up from without. But the analysis has a further result, almost as priceless as the first. It puts those of us who are Christians in a position to justify to those who are not Christians the legitimacy and the human value of resignation.

There are many reasonable men who honestly consider and denounce Christian resignation as being one of the most dangerous and soporific elements in "the opium of the people." Next to disgust with the earth, there is no attitude which the Gospel is so bitterly reproached with having fostered as that of passivity in the face of evil—a passivity which can go as far as a perverse cultivation of suffering and diminishment. As we have already said, with reference to "false detachment," this accusation, or even suspicion, is infinitely more effective, at this moment, in preventing the conversion of the world than all the objections drawn from science or philosophy. A religion which is judged to be inferior to our human ideal—in spite of the marvels by which it is surrounded—is already *condemned*. It is therefore of supreme importance for the Christian to understand and live submission to the will of God in the *active* sense which, as we have said, is the only orthodox sense.

No, if he is to practise to the full the perfection of his Christianity, the Christian must not falter in his duty to resist evil. On the contrary, during the first phase, as we have seen, he must fight sincerely and with all his strength, in union with the creative force of the world, to drive back evil—so that nothing in him or around him may be diminished. During this initial phase, the believer is the convinced ally of all those who think that humanity will not succeed unless it strives with all its might to realise its potentialities. And as we said with reference to human development, the believer is more closely tied than anyone to this great task, because in his eyes the victory of humanity over the diminishments of the world— even physical and natural—to some extent conditions the fulfillment and consummation of the quite specific Reality which he adores. As long as resistance is possible, the son of heaven will resist too—as firmly as the most worldly children of the world—everything that deserves to be scattered or destroyed.

Should he meet with defeat—the personal defeat which no human being can hope to escape in his brief single combat with forces whose order of magnitude and evolution are universal—he will, like the conquered pagan hero, still inwardly resist. Though he is stifled and constrained, his efforts will still be sustained. At that point, however, he will see a new realm of possibilities open out before him, instead of having nothing to compensate for and master his coming death except the melancholy and questionable consolation of stoicism (which, if carefully analysed, would probably prove in the end to owe its beauty and consistency to a despairing faith *in the value of sacrifice*). This hostile force that lays him low and disintegrates him can become for him a loving principle of renewal if he accepts it with faith while never ceasing to struggle against it. On the experimental plane, everything is lost. But in the realm of the supernatural, as it is called, *there is a further dimension* which allows God to achieve, *insensibly*, a mysterious reversal of evil into good. Leaving the zone of human successes and failures behind him, the Christian accedes by an effort of trust in the greater than himself to the region of supra-sensible transformations and growth. His resignation is no more than the thrust which lifts the field of his activity higher.

We have come a long way, Christianly speaking, from the justly criticised notion of "submission to the will of God," which is in danger of weakening and softening the fine steel of the human will, brandished against all the powers of darkness and diminishment. We must understand this well and cause it to be understood: to find and to do the will of God (even as we diminish and as we die) does not imply either a direct encounter or a passive attitude. I have no right to regard the evil that comes upon me through my own negligence or fault as being the touch of God.[4] I can only unite myself to the will of God (as endured passively) *when all my strength is spent*, at the point where my activity, fully extended and straining toward betterment (understood in ordinary human terms), finds itself continually counterweighted by forces tending to halt me or overwhelm me. Unless I do everything I can to advance or resist, I shall not find myself at the *required point*—I shall not submit to God as much as I might have done or as much as he wishes. If, on the contrary, I persevere courageously, I shall rejoin God across evil, deeper down than evil; I shall draw close to him; and at that moment the optimum of my "communion in resignation" necessarily coincides (by definition) with the maximum of fidelity to the human task.

Notes

1. If, in speaking of evil in this section, we do not mention sin more explicitly, it is because the aim of the following pages being solely to show how all things can help the believer to unite himself to God, there is no need to concern ourselves directly with bad actions—that is, with positive gestures of disunion. Sin only interests us here insofar as it is a weakening, a deviation caused by our personal faults (even when repented), or the pain and the scandal which the faults of others inflict on us. From this point of view it makes us suffer and can be transformed in the same way as any other suffering. That is why physical evil and moral evil are presented here, almost without distinction, in the same chapter on the passivities of diminishment.

2. Without bitterness and without revolt, of course, but with an *anticipatory tendency* to acceptance and final resignation. It is obviously difficult to separate the two "instants of nature" without to some extent distorting them in describing them. But there is this

to note: the necessity of the initial stage of resistance to evil is clear, and everyone admits it. The failure that follows on laziness, the illness contracted as a result of unjustified imprudence, could not be regarded by anyone as being the *immediate* will of God.

3. Because his perfections cannot run counter to the nature of things, and because a world, assumed to be progressing toward perfection, or "rising upward," is of its nature precisely still partially disorganised. A world without a trace or a threat of evil would be a world already consummated.

4. Though the harm which results from my negligence can become the will of God for me on condition I repent and correct my lazy or indifferent attitude of mind. Everything can be taken up again and recast in God, even one's faults.

III

A Spirituality of Creativity and Work

Charles Darwin's analysis of biological evolution, *On the Origin of Species* of 1859, set off a critical conversation between science and religious spirituality that for many churches has still not been resolved. Its appearance challenged a Christian spirituality based on classical doctrines and placed new demands on understanding the place of the human in creation. Dialogue with science opened up another way of considering Christian spirituality for our time. Thus a conversation with Catherine Keller, representing process thinking, and Pierre Teilhard de Chardin, representing a positive Christian view of evolution, provides a framework for some reflections on spirituality in a scientific age. The subtitle of this constructive interpretation puts a still finer point on the discussion. Keller and Teilhard help us to formulate a spirituality of creativity and work in a new secular world of pragmatic striving, frenetic activity, and constant innovation. How does one fully participate in this world in a way that remains consistent with Christian faith and nurtures a spiritual life?

The texts, especially as seen from the perspective of a dialogue between Christian faith and science, leave many essential questions unanswered. For example, how should one think about the relation between theology and science? Rather than pursuing that technical question, some self-evident principles can open up an intelligent discussion of spirituality in a scientific age. For example, science and faith conviction represent different kinds of knowing, each autonomous, so that neither can be reduced to the other. At the same time, each discipline is able to dialogue with and influence the other, as they do when a single individual shares a scientific and a religious consciousness. More could be said about the religious scientist, but the intent here is more constructive than apologetic: How does science help the inner vision of faith see more clearly and be more at home in the present-day world?

Keller and Teilhard provide language for a spirituality that embraces an appreciation of a new scientific conception of the world. A process view of an evolutionary world sets the framework for an appreciation of an activist culture without surrendering a contemplative or even a mystical self-consciousness. It offers a revised synthesis of a Christian spirituality that makes sense of life as it is actually lived in a constantly developing world. There is no adequate way of doing this in a short space. But the six reflections that follow represent a conversation with these authors; the discussion interprets and synthesizes their reflections into an extended statement on a spirituality of creativity and work in our scientific age.

Evolution and Process

Christianity has to reflect on how its spirituality coheres with a world of evolutionary process. We begin with this first premise. A new worldview has been introduced by science, and it makes a difference. While remaining finite, the size and age of the universe still explode the imagination. Science has changed human conceptions of the proportions of reality.

Because science limits itself to what empirical evidence provides, it has become more exact and gained more authority
over human life than in the premodern era. With technology
it has negotiated a new culture and helped form new rhythms
and patterns of everyday existence: earthly rather than
heavenly oriented, activist, instrumentalist, pragmatic, and
relentlessly developmental. This culture is gradually inter-
nalizing the environmental crisis, but the discussion here
aims at issues prior to eco-ethics and that lie beneath the
foundations of eco-spirituality: How does Christian spirituality fit into the new ways of envisioning human life in
the physical world of nature? And, reciprocally, what does
our scientifically mediated worldview teach us about the
nature of Christian spirituality?[1]

Adjusting Christian spirituality to a scientific understanding
of the world might begin by situating the human within the
natural world. For scientists, human beings are the products
of the earth. Earlier, this conviction seemed to attack several
Christian beliefs: the direct creation of the human soul, the
level of human self-consciousness, the intentional creativity
of the human species. Pierre Teilhard de Chardin was able to
integrate a developmental view of geological strata and the
evolution of hominid forms with his Christian faith in spiritual
reality and the immanence of God. Science and faith are
different ways of considering and appreciating reality, but it
makes little sense to conceive them as mutually hostile when
they stay within their boundaries. In our own time, going
right to the crux of the problem, Catherine Keller refuses to
dissociate matter and spirit. When one defines spirit as that
which is not material, the negation or transcendence of physicality still leaves whole areas of experience and value that
are real. She thus insists on their inseparability and intrinsic
entanglement.

How does one think about the mutual inherence of
spirit and matter? Whether one follows the empiricism

of Aquinas or the demand of Kant for sense data to achieve formal knowledge, one cannot quite prove the existence of the spiritual sphere. The best assurance is found in the reflective knowledge of the self in self-consciousness, but that remains subtle. By definition, one cannot have empirical evidence for the nonphysical. We are thus left with the formula that the only way we can imagine the spiritual is as connected with the physical world that embodies it. Human beings inhabit the spiritual that constitutes the human, but the spiritual remains unimaginable. The human provides the primary example of non-dual union. Other forms of spirit-talk are extrapolated from human self-consciousness itself.

Commitment to the world of matter as the embodiment of spirit represents something like a primal generative symbol for the domain of spirituality. It helps to explain the importance of this abstract discussion. The tradition of Christian thought seems to be afflicted with a spontaneous fallacy that spirit and matter can be separated or dissociated from each other. One does not have to list the separations and fruitless divided loyalties that this dichotomy has assisted. By contrast, the close association of matter and spirit opens up a new perspective on the world and Christian spirituality within it.[2]

Immanence and Transcendence

Christian spirituality has to reflect how God can be experienced as Presence and remain absolute mystery, on the immanence and transcendence of God. This statement appeals to principles from the tradition that assume new importance in a culture that has become dominated by the authority of science. One has to be able to accept the world as science explains it and find transcendent Spirit within it, not outside it or opposed to it. But because the purpose of science is to explain what appears, it carries reductionist overtones: its successes seem to explain out of existence what cannot be explained. By contrast, theology appeals to mystery because, if something could be explained in empirical terms, it would not pertain to the transcendent sphere of infinite being, that which is beyond all physical limits. The point is to be able to work through this false antithesis.

Before saying something about the contributions of science and theology to the domain of spirituality, it is important to clarify the technical character of the conversation. Science has moved beyond the everyday language of common-sense perception to become a highly critical appeal to mathematical relationships. So too, theology does not employ the language of shared common experience. Theology has become a questioning discipline that takes ordinary religious language and raises it to the level of critical interpretation, comparison with other forms of knowledge, and debate. For example, the New Testament portrays God as our Father, and Jesus taught us to address him as dwelling in heaven; but Thomas Aquinas explains why God is the pure act of being itself, and all things finite derive from God's being by creation out of nothing. Just as science defies immediate perception by saying the earth is spinning rather than the sun rising and setting, so too theology often defies spontaneous religious perception by claiming that God is not a big person in the sky and that gender applied to God makes no sense at all. These simple distinctions can go a long way in easing the tension in the conversation between a theologically mediated spirituality and a science that ignores theology and confuses it with spontaneous devotional language. They can also open up a dimension of the religious imagination to see wholly new dimensions of Christian spirituality.

A brief discussion of the transcendence and immanence of God can exemplify and test the value of a theological critique of everyday spiritual language. To affirm that God is transcendent means that God cannot be reduced to a large human-like person that the imagination spontaneously projects. The term "transcendent" constantly negates what the imagination imposes: construction of God in the image of a human being. It rejects completely anthropomorphism by affirming that God is other than all finite, created beings. As the Bible says in its own way and theologians have repeated, if it looks like a human, it is not God. The simple, subtle, and deep "negative theology" that denies everything we know about God as we conceive it only allows us to affirm God with awe and wonder.

And yet God, who is transcendent and other than any and all finite being, is claimed to be immanent within and present to the physical and the finite. This immanence is precisely not over against the material but the ground of its being. The basis of this conviction stems from a conception of God as creator, which can be understood in different ways that agree on material reality's dependence on God for its being.[3] Christian spirituality has roots that draw life from a dependence on a God that bestows value on what is other than God: finitude's intrinsic value. The only way God can be truly immanent within the human and penetrating all aspects of human existence is by being God and thus transcendent. That single insight carries with it a thoroughgoing criticism of the many forms of anthropomorphism and, not incidentally, idolatry.

God truly validates matter and guarantees the spiritual status of human existence as simultaneously the product of the earth and the consistency of physical matter. This represents no impossible contradiction or dichotomy but reflects the very structure of finite being. This conviction in its turn provides a basis for two further points that bear a strong relevance for spirituality in a culture that increasingly seems to radiate an implicit scientism. The first says that the critical view of the simultaneous immanence and transcendence of God enables Christian spirituality to retrieve the language of the mystics: God is found within the person. The many different faith traditions of the world show that spirituality can be mediated by a wide variety of finite symbols. But all of them "mediate." This means that they bear to our reflective consciousness some inner experience of the presence of the transcendent within the world and within the self.

The second point says that the simultaneity of the immanence and transcendence of God suggests that there is no profane world for the mystic because God is the within of all things. The common conception of mystical experience as an encounter with God within one's own consciousness and the prevalence of this notion suggests that all finite and material things possess the possibility of mediating transcendence to consciousness because they bear within their finitude the same power of being found within the human self. Keller opens up this perceptive outlook with her reflections on the interpenetration of spirit and matter. Teilhard appeals to a form of universal incarnation to strike a balance between reducing reality to the status of the profane and sacralizing everything.

A Hundred Years Later

Teilhard's language requires some adjustments in the light of developments in theology and ethics over the past century. Teilhard wrote during an extremely repressive era within the Catholic Church. At Vatican Council I (1870), the Catholic Church reacted against the critical "turn to the subject" in modern theology and was wary of biblical criticism and suspicious of the effects of historicity. Fifty years later, Teilhard directly suffered silencing by the Vatican. The pressure of his historical context and situation appears in his Christological language and his anthropocentrism.

The Catholic Church's rejection of the role of historical experience as a source for theology meant that Teilhard had to rely on the dogmatic Christology of his period, bolstered as it was by passages noted earlier from Colossians. As a result, he situated his spirituality within a precritical dogmatic understanding of Jesus Christ in a way that seemed to strain against its own framework. The clash in his language is evident: on one side, as a creative scientist, he appeals to a phenomenology of commitment and action; on the other, he appeals to an abstract Christ figure who often simply substitutes for "God." His Christian spirituality, like the dogmatic Christology of his period, seems to have left Jesus of Nazareth behind. To some extent this means that new issues have arisen since he wrote *The Divine Milieu* a century ago, and he must be appropriated in new ways. New issues and sensibilities opened up after Teilhard and are absent from his thinking. They do not undermine his thought, but one needs to rearrange some of his emphases in order to open the plausibility of his vision to present-day sensibility. The intellectual culture to which Teilhard now appeals has internalized not only evolution but also a critical historical consciousness. It values contemporary experience, embodies a critical appropriation of tradition, and prefers consultation and conversation to authoritarianism.

Another critique of Teilhard's language relates to his anthropocentrism, which was implanted in the tradition before the negative consequences of human exploitation became so evident. Teilhard's writing lacks the critique found in the ecospirituality movement over the past seventy years. His planet had a smaller population, and nature may have appeared as an unlimited resource. His activism does not warn against abuse of the fragility of nature's balance; we miss a sense of reservation and restriction of the impulse for dominion over the environment and other species. At this point Keller's critical reflection on the relational and responsible character of human agency needs to be highlighted.

With those cautions in mind, the power of a spirituality that draws into itself the evolutionary dynamism of reality itself can be described through the qualities of its breadth, depth, and orientation toward the future.

On the Breadth of Spirituality

An activist evolutionary spirituality allows all persons to recognize their own comprehensive spiritual identity. Thinking within the framework of evolution opens up a certain democratization of spirituality: spirituality is not esoteric but is shared by all human beings. The spirituality of action that Teilhard describes does not envision an elite set of practitioners. Everyone who acts has a spirituality. It would be appropriate to describe this as a pragmatic spirituality if the term were understood in the profound sense that persons constitute themselves by their action. Existing becomes translated into the human sphere as conscious action and intentional behavior. Teilhard is not naïve here; he corrects an easy, superficial understanding of freedom and action that misleads by depicting them as unencumbered. Freedom only exists within a context of limits and passivities. But these very passivities are the context and the means by which human beings assert their individual selves. The passivities are the platforms of activity.

The issue that underlies all consideration of spirituality revolves around that which centers it. Spirituality here refers to the way persons live their lives in relation to what they consider ultimate. More theoretically, spirituality refers to the reflective understanding of human living. In Christian and other theist spiritualities this ultimate reality is God. And the underlying question that undergirds the discussion is union with God: How are people united with God? Or, what exactly does "union" with God entail? In an activist spirituality, conscious action, in the sense of one's conscious behavior, constitutes one's operational relation with God. Union with God is forged in and by our creative action in the world, in what we do. Everyone does something. One's spirituality consists of one's actions because people fashion their identity by their behavior. That becomes clearer as certain actions and then patterns in one's behavior become more reflective and intentional.[4] Something within the human person resists the idea that the story of one's actions reveals more deeply who one is than one's immediate self-consciousness and idea of self. But critical self-reflection always shows that, not only for others but also for ourselves, our true selves are most fully revealed in our true stories.

What, then, is the union with God that is forged through practice? The question refers to something more than the ontological dependence on God as creator. There is much to be said on that premise. But we are dealing with a moral union with God. The basic structure of Christian spirituality consists in commitment to a life that reflects the values that Jesus of Nazareth taught and characterized as the rule of God. Beyond an objective moral correspondence with God's will, which always transcends human assessment, one can also appeal to a personal union with God because, when God is understood as personal, the dynamics of personal free communication of self enters into the relationship. Theology also appeals to the dynamics of ongoing creation to recognize that creaturely being entails a deep relationship of dependence in being that is being played out in one's activity. This is developed further in the next proposal.

A spirituality of action thus has three dimensions: the ontological dimension of creation that posits the immanence of God to the human subject, the forging of a moral bond by action that corresponds with the perceived will of God, and a personal dimension of the union because of the personal character of God. When these three dimensions are fused into the actuality of behavior itself, it adds up to an almost mystical union with God that is "actualized" in the sense of being made real and actual in the doing. This conception of things yields what has become known as the tradition of "contemplation in action"—that is, a conscious conviction that one is united with God in the actual behavior that makes up one's awakened hours. In other words, beyond the experience of desire to be united with God, the union is forged in one's behavior. This insight contains the grounding for both the democratization of spirituality and what is called the spirituality of everyday life.

On the Depth of Spirituality

An activist Christian evolutionary spirituality entails a commitment to something deep enough to provide meaning for every aspect of human existence. The wider the scope of the conception and application of a spirituality, the more its depth seems compromised. A spirituality of everyday life seems to level it off with the ordinary. Of course, few religious spiritualities would explicitly compromise the importance of everyone's everyday life. But given the absolute importance of each human individual, do not some conceptions of spirituality go deeper and lay out strategies for constant emulation? For example, by bringing to a focus human dependence on ultimate reality, monasticism designed patterns to keep before consciousness our deepest human relationship to God, the one who sustains our being. The question of the "depth" of a spirituality raises some basic questions. By what metric are we to judge the full meaning of an individual human life? How do people actually think about or set up criteria to assess the meaning of their lives? This becomes a critical question if one wishes to propose that a spirituality of everyday life is more than the grind that it actually is.

From the perspective of a faith tradition, for a spirituality to be deep it has to integrate the relationship with ultimacy into the logic of one's everyday action. A spirituality must strike deeper roots than any given society's or culture's standard measure for value. It cannot be measured by one's salary, or general social approval, or even an ideal of personal attributes and character. It cannot even be measured by the size of individual achievement, for no matter how one's life had been filled with passing everyday events, its meaning would still lack ultimacy. A deep spirituality has to include the way in which it is filled with ultimacy. The question then is whether everyday life can bear the character and presence of ultimacy in each person's life.

Ultimacy in Christianity points to God. An activist spirituality in the pattern of Teilhard can be clarified by the language of creation theology; creation theology gives human action in all that it does the depth dimension of the immanence of God.[5] Creation out of nothing reinforces monotheism by excluding all being outside the sphere of the one God as the source of all that is. But it does more. This conception of dependence on God also places God within the being of all that exists as the inner source of its power of being. Creation theology provides a Christian with an analogy to the Buddhist notion of non-duality. It is difficult to imagine a deeper or more intimate union of two that are inseparably one than dependence upon God's creating human existence as freedom. All being, all finite action, unfolds within the dynamic power of being whose source is God and whose effectiveness gives testimony to God's presence. God as Presence with power is often symbolized in the scriptures as the Spirit of God or God as Spirit. But as the discussion of matter and spirit showed, Spirit cannot and thus does not manifest itself outside of matter or physicality: it would have no purchase for its own self-revelation. God's Presence as a continuous creating Spirit is always manifest *in* and *through* finite reality. Thus, an egalitarian spirituality of everyday action has to include a coinherence between God's inspiring presence and each person's talents and actual fidelity to his or her work. This takes place within a universal horizon of God's comprehensive presence. God will always be interpreted according to the perceptive bias of culture, society, and individual person. But Christians have a certain standard for understanding God in the ministry of Jesus of Nazareth that insists on God's love of all of God's creation.

God as the World's Future

Evolutionary process places a new emphasis on the future as the final arbiter of the meaning and value of reality. Temporal motion adds a new factor to the question of the breadth and depth of spirituality. How should one estimate the value of reality in the face of the ultimately destructive power of time? "All is becoming" means that nothing lasts, at least, not as itself. Thich Nhat Hanh states it succinctly from a Buddhist perspective: "If you look for the self of a flower, you will see that it is empty."[6] It is empty because it is constituted by a mass of elements, an ensemble always in motion that with time degenerates into nothing of lasting identity. It ceases to be itself in becoming other things.

The consideration of time has become critical to present-day self-understanding. Once time becomes understood as a constituent of being rather than a stable container for human coming and going, consideration of the future becomes essential to self-understanding. Teilhard had a sense of this on a macro level that did not factor in the randomness of natural selection and genetics. A clear teleology accompanied his faith as a reflex that manifested itself in the gradual organic complexification of life.[7] Perhaps commitment to an ultimate goal can only be achieved by faith. Nevertheless, the evolutionary process necessarily bestows new importance on the future; life necessarily includes a sense of constantly moving into something up ahead. Every consistent spirituality will have some name for it. In Christian spirituality the future weds eschatology and resurrection into something bigger than the self that one can live for.[8]

Three themes describe a way of drawing these texts into a spirituality that gives meaning to every person's narrative by placing it within the context of an ultimate future. They are (1) an ultimate reality and value up ahead, to which (2) human beings contribute with their action, so that (3) resurrection makes sense in the existential pragmatic terms of the present. These three ideas together recapitulate a spirituality of action and bestow a larger and deeper sense of meaning for particular and concrete action, such as one's work and what one does, in the present.

First, positioning God up ahead does not remove God from the present or change the image of God that Christian spirituality culls from its scripture. The Bible provides a narrative theology rather than an abstract systematic theology; the spread of the Bible shows Israel always moving forward in time. But the phrase "God up ahead" thickens the position and relation of the human person to God. God remains an immediate divine Presence; that relationship cannot be abandoned. But God's being the horizon of an absolute future adds anticipation and exigency to steer one's life in a constructive direction. The idea of "direction" becomes a metaphor for meaningfulness.

The second point reinforces the first with a motivating conviction. The future points to a completion that makes one's present life serious and important. Work solidifies meaning by putting creativity and construction into action. Teleology might be too strong a term in the context of an evolutionary world and the openness of history, but eschatology is not. God ratifies what conforms to God's rule. Teilhard's conviction that each one contributes to the ultimate rule of God is as breathtaking as it is audacious. It seems to have given his own life a sense of direction, stability, and serenity beneath the turmoil. The idea of teleology does not have to be abandoned, but it needs to be nuanced in a universe of evolutionary process. For example, on the material level the idea of "complexification" of life in its granular detail involves an irregular process of aborted dead-ends rather than a smooth straight line. Ultimately conviction about the teleological structure of reality remains an object of faith and hope.

Third, these two points supply a framework for understanding the logic of Christian belief in resurrection. There can be no comprehension of the meaningfulness of Jesus' resurrection outside of an intrinsic desire for the ultimate meaningfulness of one's own life. Faith in Jesus' resurrection is hope for our own and is no less than the inner logic of spirituality itself: the quest for the ultimate meaning of one's life within life itself. This is not the place for a discourse on the theology of resurrection. But the idea of the "creative memory" of God, which means exactly that God's memory also sustains in being, resolves the dilemma of fanciful images of either a human spirit without a body or a physical temporal body that is not a self.

* * * *

As a conclusion to this extrapolation of an activist spirituality of work and creativity from the writings of Keller and Teilhard, a creative interpretation of a medieval maxim on the goodness of God might be appropriate. It was said that "*bonum est diffusivum sui*," the good communicates its own goodness.[9] The maxim has several meanings. When it is applied to God, it has an ontological meaning that reaffirms the story of Genesis that God is the creator of all and all of it is good. It means that the desirability or attractiveness that defines the good communicates itself to others, and they desire it. Together those two senses of the saying help explain the logic of an activist Christian spirituality. The value and importance of a particular life has two dimensions. The first is given it by creation; the second is seized by the mind, internalized into commitment, and constructively acted out. The values to which persons commit themselves accrue to themselves; and, by their action, persons contribute that value back to the common good to last eternally.

Notes

1. Scientific reductionism, beginning with an instrumentalization of the imagination, is certainly worthy of critique. But after it, we are still amazed by the power of collective science in our world and our lives. The point of this reflection is not to offer a religious critique of it, but to see where it may positively influence Christian spirituality.

2. Current theology draws attention to bodiliness, and so it should. But that language too risks reduction. When it runs its course, we will have to insist again on the spiritual character of the human person and not bodies.

3. Keller's theology of creation out of infinitely potential chaos and the tradition of creation out of nothing are not the same. But the differences do not add up to a conflictual contradiction relative to the simultaneous immanence and transcendence of God; they rather emphasize different aspects of it. In Keller's case, an absolute refusal to imagine a separation between God and the world's materiality; in the tradition, the transcendence of God is despite the actual coinherence.

4. The idea of intentionality is slippery because there are so many different levels of reflective self-awareness. Even ignorance can be a knowing unknowing or a deliberate ignorance. At points like this the generalizations do not penetrate to the actuality of any given case.

5. Sometimes Teilhard makes the following point with the language of creation theology, but more often he appeals to the cosmic Christ or to the Spirit of God. The language of creation gives it wider application.

6. This teaching of the Buddha is to assist one in not becoming attached to temporal concepts and doctrines. Thich Nhat Hanh, *Living Buddha, Living Christ* (New York: Riverhead, 1995), 54–55.

7. The term "teleology" can have a nontemporal sense as, for example, the fitting together of organic elements and functions. The clearest temporal sense of teleology comes from human consciousness when an actor acts with the intention of achieving a goal. This provides the basis for imagining the whole universe acting out the intended goal of the creator. Ideas of contingency

and evolution's randomness interrupt the simple clarity of this example and force deeper reflection.

8. Eschatology, consideration of the end of time, is not unrelated to teleology, but it does not stress as strongly purposeful relationships between what happens in time and the end of time.

9. The maxim is neo-Platonic, suggesting cosmic emanation. But Dionysius the Areopagite offers a beautiful comparison of God diffusing goodness as the sun communicates its light to illumine all things (*The Divine Names*, Chap. 4, Paragraph 4). Aquinas frequently appealed to Dionysius and expressed similar ideas in his *Summa Theologiae* I, q. 6, a. 4; I, q. 19, a. 2. He raises the phrase to the level of a maxim by reading it as a natural tendency and ascribes a comprehensive meaning to it: God spreads goodness effectively by creating it, by exemplifying it, and, with teleological intent, as a goal to provide a desirableness that attracts creatures to itself.

Further Reading

Cuénot, Claude. *Teilhard de Chardin: A Biographical Study*. Edited by René Hague. Baltimore: Helicon Press, 1965. [An early biography translated from the French by Vincent Colimore that ably introduces the man and his work.]

Deane-Drummond, Celia, ed. *Pierre Teilhard de Chardin on People and Planet*. Oakville, Conn.: Equinox, 2006. [This collection of essays provides interpretations of Teilhard's mystical vision of the whole of reality, including his views of one planet, one people, searching for ways of living together while balancing scientific knowledge with ethical and spiritual responsibility.]

Duffy, Kathleen. *Teilhard's Mysticism: Seeing the Inner Face of Evolution*. Maryknoll, N.Y.: Orbis, 2014. [This book finds in Teilhard's early writings the wellsprings of his spirituality in a mystical engagement with matter and God's spiritual presence in it.]

Grim, John, and Mary Evelyn Tucker. *Biography*. American Teilhard Association. http://teilharddechardin.org/index.php /biography. [This very short biography traces the highlights of Teilhard's development and his career and how he internalized his distinctive Christian vision of our world and life in it.]

Kearney, Richard. "Beyond the Impossible: Dialogue with Catherine Keller." *Reimagining the Sacred: Richard Kearney Debates God*. New York: Columbia University Press, 2016 (online): 46–75. [This long conversation brings out many dimensions of the experience of God behind Keller's work and implied spirituality.]

Keller, Catherine. *Cloud of the Impossible: Negative Theology and Planetary Entanglement*. Maryknoll, N.Y.: Orbis, 2021 (online). [Keller explores what we really know relative to ultimate things: How do we live in apophatic reverence for everything when it is so profoundly entangled? Possibility always mingles with impossibility so that deepest faith is our uncertainty because what exists is in process.]

King, Ursula, ed. *Pierre Teilhard de Chardin: Selected Writings*. Maryknoll, N.Y.: Orbis, 1999). [This collection of texts gives a broader view of Teilhard's spirituality by arranging texts from across his writings according to themes of God's immanence to life in the world.]

———, ed. *Rediscovering Teilhard's Fire*. Philadelphia: Saint Joseph's University Press, 2010. [A collection of essays on Teilhard's thought that includes reflections on his cosmic spirituality, relation to science, evolution, process thought, and aesthetics.]

Salmon, James, and John Farina, eds. *The Legacy of Pierre Teilhard de Chardin*. Mahwah, N.J.: Paulist Press, 2011. [Scientists and theologians contribute to this collection of essays interpreting nature and influence of Teilhard's contribution to Christian thought.]

Teilhard de Chardin, Pierre. *Writings in Time of War*. New York: Harper & Row, 1968. [These essays written by Teilhard between 1916 and 1919 are arranged by topics and give an intimate picture of the developing spirituality of Teilhard.]

About the Series

The volumes of this series provide readers direct access to important voices in the history of the faith. Each of the writings has been selected, first, for its value as a historical document that captures the cultural and theological expression of a figure's encounter with God. Second, as "classics," the primary materials witness to the "transcendent" in a way that has proved potent for the formation of Christian life and meaning beyond the particularities of the setting of its authorship.

Recent renewed interest in mysticism and spirituality have encouraged new movements, contributed to a growing body of therapeutic-moral literature, and inspired the recovery of ancient practices from Church tradition. However, the meaning of the notoriously slippery term "spirituality" remains contested. The many authors who write on the topic have different frameworks of reference, divergent criteria of evaluation, and competing senses of the principal sources or witnesses. This situation makes it important to state the operative definition used in this series. *Spirituality is the way people live in relation to what they consider to be ultimate.* So defined, spirituality is a universal phenomenon: everyone has one, whether they can fully articulate it or not. Spirituality emphasizes lived experience and concrete expression of one's principles, attitudes, and convictions, whether rooted in a defined tradition or not. It includes not only interiority and devotional practices but also the real outworkings of people's ideas and values. Students of spirituality examine the way that a person or group conceives of a meaningful existence through the practices that orient them toward their horizon of deepest meaning. What animates their life? What motivates their truest desires? What sustains them and instructs them? What provides for them a vision of the good life? How do they define and pursue truth? And how do they imagine and work to realize their shared vision of a good society?

The "classic" texts and authors presented in these volumes, though they represent the diversity of Christian traditions, define their ultimate value in God through Christ by the Spirit. They share a conviction that the Divine has revealed God's self in history through Jesus Christ. God's self-communication, in turn, invites a response through faith to participate in an intentional life of self-transcendence and to co-labor with the Spirit in manifesting the reign of God. Thus, *Christian spirituality refers to the way that individuals or social entities live out their encounter with God in Jesus Christ by a life in the Spirit.*

Christian spirituality necessarily involves a hermeneutical task. Followers of Christ set about the work of integrating knowledge and determining meaning through an interpretative process that refracts through different lenses: the life of Jesus, the witness of the scripture, the norms of the faith community, the traditions and social structures of one's heritage, the questions of direct experience, the criteria of the academy and other institutions that mediate truthfulness and viability, and personal conscience. These seemingly competing authorities can leave contemporary students of theology with more quandaries than clarity. Thus, this series has anticipated this challenge with an intentional structure that will guide students through their encounter with classic texts. Rather than providing commentary on the writings themselves, this series invites the audience to engage the texts with an informed sense of the context of their authorship and a dialog with the text that begins a conversation about how to make the text meaningful for theology, spirituality, and ethics in the present.

Most of the readers of these texts will be familiar with critical historical methods which enable an understanding of scripture in the context within which it was written. However, many people read scripture according to the common sense understanding of their ordinary language. This almost inevitably leads to some degree of misinterpretation. The Bible's content lies embedded in its cultural context, which is foreign to the experience of contemporary believers. Critical historical study enables a reader to get closer to an authentic past meaning by explicitly attending to the historical period, the situation of the author, and other particularities of the composition of the text. For example, one would miss the point of the story of the "Good Samaritan" if one did not recognize that the first-century Palestinian conflict between Jews and Samaritans makes the hero of the Jewish parable an enemy and an unlikely model of virtue! Something deeper than a simple offer of neighborly love is going on in this text.

However, the more exacting the critical historical method becomes, the greater it increases the distance between the text and the present-day reader. Thus, a second obstacle to interpreting classics for contemporary theology, ethics, and spirituality lies in a bias that texts embedded in a world so different from today cannot carry an inner authority for present life. How can we find something both true and relevant for faith today in a witness that a critical historical method determines to be in some measure alien? The basic problem has two dimensions: how do we appreciate the past witnesses of our tradition on their own terms, and, once we have, how can we learn from something so dissimilar?

Most Christians have some experience navigating this dilemma through biblical interpretation. Through Church membership, Christians have gained familiarity with scriptural language, and preaching consistently applies its content to daily life. But beyond the Bible, a long history of cultural understanding, linguistic innovation, doctrinal negotiations, and shifting patterns of practices has added layer upon layer of meaning to Christian spirituality. Veiled in unfamiliar grammar, images, and politics, these texts may appear as cultural artifacts suitable only for scholarly treatments. How can a modern student of theology understand a text cloaked in an unknown history and still encounter in it a transcendent faith that animates life in the present? Many historical and theological aspects of Christian spirituality that are still operative in communities of faith are losing traction among swathes of the population, especially younger generations. Their premises have been called into question; the metaphors are dead; the symbols appear unable to mediate grace; and the ideas appear untenable. For example, is the human species really saved by the blood of Jesus on the cross? What does it mean to be resurrected from the dead? How does the Spirit unify if the church is so divided? On the other hand, the positive experiences and insights that accrued over time and added depth to Christian spirituality are being lost because they lack critical appropriation for our time. For example, has asceticism been completely lost in present-day spirituality or can we find meaning for it today? Do the mystics live in another universe, or can we find mystical dimensions in religious consciousness today? Does monasticism bear meaning for those who live outside the walls?

This series addresses these questions with a three-fold strategy. The historical first step introduces the reader to individuals who represent key ideas, themes, movements, doctrinal developments, or remarkable distinctions in theology, ethics, or spirituality. This first section will equip readers with a sense of the context of the authorship and a grammar for understanding the text.

Second, the reader will encounter the witnesses in their own words. The selected excerpts from the authors' works have exercised great influence in the history of Christianity.

Letting these texts speak for themselves will enable readers to encounter the wisdom and insight of these classics anew. Equipped with the necessary background and language from the introduction, students of theology will bring the questions and concerns of their world into contact with the world of the authors. This move personalizes the objective historical context and allows the existential character of the classic witness to appear. The goal is not the study of the exact meaning of ancient texts, as important as that is. That would require a task outside the scope of this series. Recommended readings will be provided for those who wish to continue digging into this important part of interpretation. These classic texts are not presented as comprehensive representations of their authors but as statements of basic characteristic ideas that still have bearing on lived experience of faith in the twenty-first century. The emphasis lies on existential depth of meaning rather than adequate representation of an historical period which can be supplemented by other sources.

Finally, each volume also offers a preliminary interpretation of the relevance of the author and text for the present. The methodical interpretations seek to preserve the past historical meanings while also bringing them forward in a way that is relevant to life in a technologically developed and pluralistic secular culture. Each retrieval looks for those aspects that can open realistic possibilities for viable spiritual meaning in current lived experience. In the unfolding wisdom of the many volumes, many distinct aspects of the Christian history of spirituality converge into a fuller, deeper, more far-reaching, and resonant language that shows what in our time has been taken for granted, needs adjustment, or has been lost (or should be). The series begins with fifteen volumes but, like Cassian's *Conferences*, the list may grow.

About the Editors

ROGER HAIGHT is a Visiting Professor at Union Theological Seminary in New York. He has written several books in the area of fundamental theology. A graduate of the University of Chicago, he is a past president of the Catholic Theological Society of America.

ALFRED PACH III is an Associate Professor of Medical Sciences and Global Health at the Hackensack Meridian School of Medicine. He has a Ph.D. from the University of Wisconsin in Madison and an MDiv in Psychology and Religion from Union Theological Seminary.

AMANDA AVILA KAMINSKI is an Assistant Professor of Theology at Texas Lutheran University, where she also serves as Director of the program in Social Innovation and Social Entrepreneurship. She has written extensively in the area of Christian spirituality.

Past Light on Present Life:
Theology, Ethics, and Spirituality

Roger Haight, SJ, Alfred Pach III,
and *Amanda Avila Kaminski,* series editors

Available titles:

Western Monastic Spirituality: John Cassian, Caesarius of Arles,
    and Benedict
On the Medieval Structure of Spirituality: Thomas Aquinas
Grace and Gratitude: Spirituality in Martin Luther
Spirituality of Creation, Evolution, and Work: Catherine Keller
    and Pierre Teilhard de Chardin
Spiritualities of Social Engagement: Walter Rauschenbusch
    and Dorothy Day

Ingram Content Group UK Ltd.
Milton Keynes UK
UKHW040720170323
418699UK00009B/284

9 781531 503833